HOCKEY ADDICT'S GUIDE
TORONTO

THE SPORT GALLERY

HOCKEY ADDICT'S GUIDE
TORONTO

WHERE TO EAT, DRINK & PLAY THE ONLY GAME THAT MATTERS

EVAN GUBERNICK

THE COUNTRYMAN PRESS

A division of W. W. Norton & Company

Independent Publishers Since 1923

All photographs by Evan Gubernick, unless otherwise indicated.
Pages 13 (School), 18, 19, 29, 36 (Town Barber), 39, 44 (June Records), 53, 59, 60, 62, 74–75, 78 (Shoxs Billiards Lounge), 79, 82–83, 86, 87, 88–89, 94, 98 (Hair of the Dog), 100 (Ozzy's Burgers), 103, 116, 119, 129, 132 (Detroit Eatery), 138, 140–141, 144: Andre Legaspi; pages 13 (Dog & Bear), 15, 47 (Hurricane's Roadhouse), 50 (The Dock Ellis), 51, 67, 71, 78 (Shaky's), 80, 96 (Black Camel), 97, 98 (The Anndore House), 100 (Shark Club), 110, 111, 118, 120, 121, 127, 130, 131, 132 (The Wren), 154, 155, 158, 160–161: Sabrina Leeder/BiA Photography; page 16: © Graig Abel/Getty Images; page 17: © Lee Balterman/Sports Illustrated/Getty Images; pages 26–27, 139: © Bruce Bennett Studios/ Getty Images; pages 42–43, 66: © Kevin Sousa/NLHI via Getty Images; page 61, 72–73: © Denis Brodeur/Getty Images; page 81: Nickel 9 Distillery; pages 84–85: © Melchior DiGiacomo/Getty Images; page 90: © Lucas Oleniuk/Toronto Star via Getty Images; page 101: © Doug Griffin/Toronto Star via Getty Images; page 104: © Toronto Star Archives/Toronto Star via Getty Images; page 109: © Dave Abel/Getty Images; pages 122–123: © Ron Bull/Toronto Star via Getty Images; pages 134–135: © Chris So/Toronto Star via Getty Images; pages 142–143: Mike Wilson/Ultimate Leafs Fan; page 145: Antonio Lennert/Surf the Greats; page 153: Graham Williamson/Gitch Sportswear

For information about permission to reproduce selections from this book, write to Permissions, The Countryman Press, 500 Fifth Avenue, New York, NY 10110

For information about special discounts for bulk purchases, please contact W. W. Norton Special Sales at specialsales@wwnorton.com or 800-233-4830

Manufacturing by Versa Press

Library of Congress Cataloging-in-Publication Data

Names: Gubernick, Evan, author.
Title: Hockey addicts guide Toronto : where to eat, drink & play the only game that matters / Evan Gubernick.
Description: New York, NY : The Countryman Press, A division of W. W. Norton & Company, [2019] | Series: Hockey addict city guides | Includes bibliographical references and index.
Identifiers: LCCN 2018056248 | ISBN 9781682681527 (pbk. : alk. paper)
Subjects: LCSH: Hockey—Ontario—Toronto—Guidebooks. | Toronto (Ont.)— Guidebooks. | Ontario—Guidebooks.
Classification: LCC GV848.6.C45 G83 2019 | DDC 796.962/6409713541—dc23
LC record available at https://lccn.loc.gov/2018056248

The Countryman Press
www.countrymanpress.com

A division of W. W. Norton & Company, Inc.
500 Fifth Avenue, New York, NY 10110
www.wwnorton.com

10 9 8 7 6 5 4 3 2 1

Contents

The Warm-Up

NO CURE EXISTS IF HOCKEY GETS IN YOUR BLOOD. And it's not a seasonal condition, it's a daily obsession. Hourly, even. An obvious symptom: Your life becomes a diversion from hockey, not the other way around. While (relatively) manageable at home, should you venture out of town, you're lost and you know it. Your radar is jammed. Our solution: One city at a time, we're creating a series of guides with recommendations made by those who share your passion for the only sport that matters—including food, drink, lodging, and, of course, where to skate. The guides are a product of local hockey communities, curated and written by your fellow puck heads, from fans to beer leaguers, with tips from a few industry pros sprinkled in. Hockey, at its core, is tribal, connecting us to our cities and to each other, so trust your tribe when you leave your home ice.

HOW THE GUIDE IS ORGANIZED Like the game itself, think of this guide as organized chaos. A few set plays off the faceoff, a general gameplan, and then it's on. We've divided the city into "Hubs," must-see places for the hockey-afflicted, and listed additional spots to check out nearby. Think of these recommendations as mini walking tours—and by "walking" we sometimes mean taking the subway or grabbing a Lyft. Your choice. And last, we give you a little local hockey history, so if you wind up talking to a local, maybe you'll have a clue. This isn't a typical guidebook. We've avoided the usual ratings, prices, and comparisons. (See Yelp for that.) If it's in here, we like it. We have one map: it's crude, but—like a coach's scribblings—it does its job (sorry, not sorry). Do we miss some obvious hot spots? Probably. Do we lead you down some strange alleys? For sure. But this is a conversation, and we're the only ones talking. If you know of a spot we missed, tell us. Listen, this guide won't solve all your problems. You're still going to have that nightmare where you're sitting on the bench with bare feet. But this guide should help you feel at home in Toronto.

THE HOCKEY ADDICT'S GUIDE TO TORONTO Hockey is absolutely everywhere, with more rinks than we knew possible, so we've decided to concentrate on the city of Toronto, with occasional ventures out into the Greater Toronto Area (GTA). A few things you should know: 1) This is a city of distinct neighborhoods, whose personalities change within a few blocks. 2) The weather is better than you think. 3) The locals are even nicer than you think . . . 4) considering that the Leafs haven't won a Cup since there were six teams in the league. 5) Colorful characters fill the city's hockey past, like former Leafs owner Harold Ballard who, having booked the Beatles to play at The Gardens, disabled all the water fountains and turned up the heat so as to sell more triple-priced sodas.

HOWARD SCRUTON

COULSON

DAVE TROTTIER

BARRY MacKENZIE

SCOTT McLELLAN

KEVIN DINEEN

JOHN MAROIS
DECEASED

ROB DECOURCY
DECEASED

HARVEY TENO

JOHN ENGLISH

DON WILLSON
DECEASED

SOME ST. MICHAEL'S ALUMNI

CHESSWOOD
ARENA

ST. MICHAEL'S
SCHOOL ARENA

MATTAMY
ATHLETIC
CENTRE

TED REEVE
COMMUNITY
ARENA

THE SPORT
GALLERY

SID SMITH
RINK

99
WAYNE
GRETZKY'S
TORONTO

HOCKEY HALL
OF FAME

TORONTO
HOCKEY
REPAIR

SCOTIABANK
ARENA

COCA-COLA
COLISEUM

MASTERCARD
CENTRE FOR
HOCKEY
EXCELLENCE

TOR
Hubs

tor hub

COCA-COLA COLISEUM

45 MANITOBA DR. • 416.263.3900

Home ice of the Toronto Marlies, the Leafs' AHL affiliate, this arena sits pretty much dead center between the MasterCard Centre (where both teams practice) and Scotiabank Arena (the Leafs' home ice). Given that only three NHL teams share a city with their minor league squad, this proximity creates a somewhat unique opportunity for current Leafs to sneak a look at who might be replacing them in the lineup. Previously named the Ricoh Coliseum, a nearly 100-year-old structure outfitted for hockey in 2003, its naming rights were sold to Coca-Cola a month after the Marlies won their first-ever Calder Cup in 2018, so it's only a matter of time before the obvious nickname of "Colaseum" takes hold. In addition to a few 11 a.m. "school-day-game" puck drops (only in Canada is hockey an excuse to watch AHL hockey), the rink is also available to rent for private games. So assemble a roster, put word out to 8,300 of your closest friends to watch, and get after it.

SKATE
THE BENTWAY

250 FORT YORK BLVD. • 416.304.0222

The roof was already there, and by roof we mean the Gardiner Expressway, a major artery running along the southern edge of the city where, 48 feet below, now sits a 700-foot-long skate trail in the shape of what locals call "a lazy figure eight." Opened as the first phase of a larger urban parkification of previously ignored postindustrial space, the trail offers free skating with never-before-appreciated views of the fast-growing downtown area. The entire Bentway project will eventually span over a mile and include amenities for a wide array of cultural activities, in addition to the obviously essential recreational one already created.

ROAD TRIP PICK

ANDRE LEGASPI

EAT
SCHOOL

70 FRASER AVE.
416.588.0005

Brunch is important business in Toronto. For millennials in the industrial Liberty Village, School is the main spot for midmorning refueling. Every weekend morning, a line of fashionable and hungry 20-somethings forms out the door and around the corner, making the block feel like it was plucked out of Park Slope or Williamsburg. The joint offers lunch and dinner as well, but it's mainly known for creative weekend morning offerings.

EAT & DRINK
DOG & BEAR

1100 QUEEN ST. W
647.352.8601

Though free from British rule since 1931, Canada recognizes the Queen as their constitutional head of state, and as such, by royal decree, access to decent bangers and mash within the GTA is guaranteed, along with a $15 CAD fish & chips + pint special every Friday.

EAT
MILDRED TEMPLE KITCHEN
85 HANNA AVE.
416.588.5695

The original incarnation of this spot was a restaurant called Mildred Pierce (named for the title character of a 1945 film noir who owns a string of restaurants) that closed in 2007 after an 18-year run. Brunch is the focus here, though they don't accept reservations on weekends, so expect a line—half of which is definitely getting the pancakes and probably a sweet "Mrs. Biederhof's Blueberry Buttermilk Pancakes" t-shirt.

EAT & DRINK
PARTS & LABOUR
1566 QUEEN ST. W
416.588.7750

A neighborhood hardware store in a previous life, this cavernous restaurant outfitted in found-object decor, with large communal tables, a bar, and downstairs music venue is almost a decade old, so it can no longer be called "trendy."

EAT & DRINK
THE CRAFT BRASSERIE
107 ATLANTIC AVE.
416.535.2337

Lower your gaze and you'll spot some of the 120 taps on hand, with a focus on local Ontario microbrews.

Kyle Baun

TORONTO MARLIES
'17–'18

Acquired by the Maple Leafs in February 2018, Baun has spent his brief tenure in the organization with the Marlies of the AHL. His grandfather Bobby Baun was a three-time Stanley Cup champion with the Leafs.

EAT

CHUBBY'S JAMAICAN KITCHEN

104 PORTLAND ST.
416.792.8105
It's got a cool, island vibe to it.

GUSTO 101

101 PORTLAND ST.
416.504.9669
A relaxing Italian place with a great rooftop patio.

BUTTER CHICKEN FACTORY

556 PARLIAMENT ST.
416.964.7583
Good authentic Indian food.

PAI

18 DUNCAN ST.
416.901.4724
Good Thai food. I really like that Toronto has so many different types of cultures. I try to take advantage of that.

ZEN JAPANESE RESTAURANT

7634 WOODBINE AVE., MARKHAM
905.604.7211
This used to be a go-to place for my family.

PLAY

CANLAN ICE SPORTS

159 DYNAMIC DR.
SCARBOROUGH • 416.412.0404
I skate here a lot in the summer, partially because of convenience, and also because one of my coaches has a gym here. A great rink.

POOL, ETC.

THE REC ROOM

255 BREMNER BLVD.
416.815.0086
Pool tables, video games—a fun way to kill time.

HANG

TRINITY BELLWOODS PARK

It's a really nice park. There's always a lot going on in the summertime.

INTERVIEW BY ROB DEL MUNDO

SCARBOROUGH BLUFFS

Near where I grew up, with a lot of paths and trails to walk. And Bluffers Park Marina is a pretty spot.

FIRST HOCKEY MEMORY

When I was six, at the closing of Maple Leaf Gardens (1999), they had a bunch of TimBits [kids aged four to nine] hockey players go out. For that specific game, they had alumni with grandsons and granddaughters, and I just happened to be there. I had been exposed to a few other special events, but that was the first time it really sunk in.

HIS GRANDFATHER BOBBY BAUN

If you're not from Toronto, maybe you've heard the name, but you don't quite associate it with his famous goal. But, me being from Toronto and people knowing me from Toronto, I'm definitely asked about him a lot.

Bob Baun
TORONTO MAPLE LEAFS
'56–'67, '70–'73

Famously scored in overtime to win game six of the '64 Cup final after having fractured his ankle earlier in the game. Injury kept him on the bench for the '67 Cup win and he didn't celebrate with the team, the result of his conflict with GM Punch Imlach over a raise the previous season. Baun was left unprotected in the 1967 NHL Expansion Draft, and was selected by the Oakland Seals.

ROAD TRIP PICK

ANDRE LEGASPI

EAT
DOOMIE'S

1263 QUEEN ST. W
416.536.4692

Vegans and vegetarians looking for meatless options should look no further than Doomie's—unless you're looking for *healthy* vegan options. These folks spurn the salad and crank out comfort food classics that are both plant-based and heavy on the calories. Even the most voracious carnivore, especially after downing a couple of their tasty cocktails, wouldn't be any the wiser after scarfing down their "chicken" fingers, animal-free animal fries, or vegan asada chimichangas.

SLEEP
MAKING WAVES BOATEL

539 QUEENS QUAY W
647.403.2764

From June through September (okay, not exactly hockey season), this boat, a 65-foot private yacht, morphs into a three-room bed and breakfast. The owners, Diane and Ted Greene, live aboard the Boatel in Toronto during the summer and then cruise south to the Bahamas for the winter. These folks have it figured out.

EAT / DRINK
BRAZEN HEAD IRISH PUB
165 E. LIBERTY ST.
416.535.8787

With no Leafs game on the schedule, we were curious when we noticed some serious pregaming spilling out of this pub. We realized it was for the Toronto Wolfpack, the local rugby team whose home "paddock" is at nearby Lamport Stadium. As it turns out, their away games are, in fact, far away. The world's first transatlantic rugby team (their opponents are based in England and France) began play in 2017, and as all this was patiently explained to us, we noticed "Guinness-braised ribs" on the menu and any interest we had in the intricacies of rugby vanished.

tor hub
WAYNE GRETZKY'S TORONTO

99 BLUE JAYS WAY, TORONTO
416.348.0099

●●●●●

From nearby Brantford, Ontario—about an hour south of the city—the Great One never played for his hometown Leafs (though he brought some Cups to a prairie town 2,000 miles to the west), he did open what has become a local institution in the heart of downtown. Basically a blown-out man cave, with 50 screens, a substantial food and drink menu, enough 99 memorabilia to warrant a tour, and an in-house Wayne-themed apparel and accessory shop. A popular spot for crowds headed to and from the nearby Rogers Centre (home to the Blue Jays), Gretzky himself has been known to frequent his eatery when in town (we hear he's partial to the restaurant's Oasis Rooftop Patio), so keep your head up to catch a glimpse or, better yet, grab a beer with the greatest player to ever lace up.

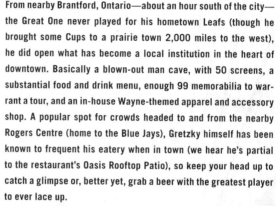

SITE
CN TOWER
301 FRONT ST. W

Every city needs an icon to slap on a fitted cap or coffee mug, and what a bold one this is, the tallest freestanding structure in the Western Hemisphere. Even if you never take the 58-second elevator ride to the top to see a pilot's face up close, the structure still has its purpose. Wherever you are in the city, this tower always seems over your shoulder, making it virtually impossible to get lost, as you always have the perfect milepost to gauge your location.

CULTURE
ART GALLERY OF ONTARIO
317 DUNDAS ST. W • 416.979.6648

The structure, originally built in 1900, received a major facelift in 2004 by world renowned architect and Toronto native Frank Gehry, his first work in Canada—all for a tidy $276 million CAD, clearly a hometown discount. Free on Wednesday nights, the museum contains a collection of close to 95,000 works spanning centuries and media types.

MY PICKS

Greg Collins

OWNER, GRIT, INC.
Only a Toronto native of a certain age could quietly share that Mike Keenan, the notoriously strict NHL coach, was his gym teacher (that must have been pleasant). Currently an old-timers (40+) skater, he had to walk home from the rink as a kid, which is where he got the inspiration for Grit's innovative "backpack" hockey bag.

EAT / DRINK / SKATE
PENALTY BOX AT WESTWOOD ARENA
90 WOODBINE DOWNS BLVD.
ETOBICOKE • 416.675.7604
One of my favorite old rinks, with a great spot to grab a beer and a bite.

COFFEE SHOP
THE SENATOR RESTAURANT
249 VICTORIA ST. • 416.364.7517
Filmmakers and designers eat here for breakfast.

COMICS
SILVER SNAIL
329 YONGE ST. • 416.593.0889
The best comic store in Toronto.

SITE
THE DISTILLERY DISTRICT
A reclaimed area formerly known as the Gooderham & Worts Distillery.

GEAR
PRO HOCKEY LIFE
1 BASS PRO MILLS DR. C3
CONCORD
905.669.9088
The biggest hockey superstore in Canada.

TORONTO HOCKEY REPAIR
1592 BLOOR ST. W
416.533.1791
One of the last independent hockey stores in Toronto.

SHOP
ADRIFT
116 SPADINA AVE. • 416.515.0550

What began as a more traditional skate shop in Kensington Market has elevated (or sold out, depending on your stance) to a more fashion-forward approach in their Spadina Avenue location. Carrying a wide selection of urban lifestyle brands from all over the globe, stocking skate apparel and footwear, they keep a few boards on hand to maintain their cred in the community.

BEER
LEAGUE
PICKS
JOSH COOPER

EAT
416 SNACK BAR
181 BATHURST ST.
416.364.9320

TERRONI
720 QUEEN ST. W
416.504.1992

PING-PONG
SPIN TORONTO
461 KING ST. W • 416.599.7746

Looking for a lost ping-pong ball is a bit like locating this place. A few twists and turns, so much so that adjacent buildings have signs telling you that "You are NOT at Spin." The upside is that once you get there, finding your wandering ball is not a problem. The floor is littered with them. Grab another from the basket and keep ponging. Or pinging.

SHOP
EXCLUCITY
552 QUEEN ST. W • 416.815.8887

Founded in Montreal, this shop's Toronto location opened in 2015 and quickly earned its cred in the sneaker community. A second floor began as a reveal space for new products (such as an Adidas takeover during NBA All-Star weekend 2016) and then evolved to become Status, a high-end annex to the original street-level shop. A second Toronto location on Yonge Street opened early February 2018.

Tim Horton
TORONTO MAPLE LEAFS
'52–'70

A mid-size, brutally strong defenseman with a storied Leafs career, including four Cups, Tim Horton's name conjures a logo more than a memory, and he only had himself to blame. Salaries being a fraction of today's, he knew he had to plan for life after hockey. Following failed attempts with a car dealership and a burger joint, Horton opened his first Tim Horton Doughnut Shop in Hamilton, Ontario, in 1964. By the time of his tragic death 10 years later, at the age of 44, killed in a car crash driving home to Buffalo (he was a Sabre by then) from a game at Maple Leaf Gardens, he had grown his business to 39 locations. During his career, he managed to play in 486 straight games, a record that stood for almost four decades. It was no surprise that the Leafs retired his number 7 after his 20-year career in Toronto. What may have been a more profound indicator of his impact on a team was when the Sabres retired his number 2, after playing in only 124 regular season games for them. Surely a record that will never be broken.

David Shoalts

TORONTO'S *THE
GLOBE AND MAIL*
COLUMNIST AND
AUTHOR OF *TALES
FROM THE TORONTO
MAPLE LEAFS
LOCKER ROOM*
A sense of humor seems
necessary to be a Leafs
fan, but what's needed if
you've covered them for
more than 30 years as a
journalist? To take the
plunge and become a
stand-up comic.

Renowned hockey
scribe for *The Globe and
Mail* since 1984, who
also plays beer league in
Bolton (about an hour
northwest of down-
town) and a weekly
shinny game at Moss
Park, Shoalts' interest
in comedy was initially
limited to checking out
the occasional comedy
club while on the road
for the paper. He never
considered getting up
on stage until a friend
took a comedy course at
Second City, which cul-
minated with each stu-
dent doing a five-minute
set at Absolute Comedy
on Yonge Street. "I was
surprised, they were

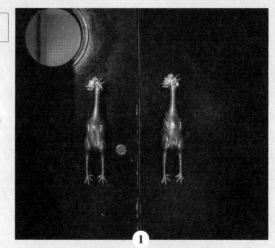

really good," he recalls.
"I signed up on the
spot."

After completing
the seven-week course,
Shoalts made his debut,
and now he hits the
comedy scene, either as
a performer or audience
member, whenever time
allows.

A few of his favor-
ite spots to watch and
perform:

YUK YUKS [1]

224 RICHMOND ST. W
416.967.6431
Shows every night except
Monday, and weekends they
bring in top talent. Two shows
on Tuesday nights, the first
is students from the comedy
course at Humber College

and the second is a more
standard amateur night.

ABSOLUTE COMEDY

2335 YONGE ST. • 416.486.7700
On Wednesdays they have an
amateur night that's pretty
good. For $8 CAD you get
three to five amateurs plus a
headliner or two. A cut above
open mic.

COMEDY KAPOW AT 120 DINER

120 CHURCH ST. • 416.792.7725
On Friday nights, there's a
really good show at 120 Diner,
which is an actual diner.
Same kind of amateur night
as Absolute Comedy and Yuk
Yuks, but with the crowd and
the food, it's really fun. Grab
tickets in advance because
they're often sold out.

LISTEN

THE HORSESHOE
TAVERN

370 QUEEN ST. W
416.598.4226

The granddaddy of Toronto
live music, so to speak.
Everyone has played here.
Sweaty late nights . . .
with ears buzzing from
melodious air. Immortal-
ized in The Tragically Hip
song "Bobcaygeon": "That
night in Toronto with its
checkerboard floors."

CULTURE
GRAFFITI ALLEY
ENTER BETWEEN QUEEN ST. W
AND RICHMOND ST.

The street art scene in Toronto is on the rise, so if you're strolling down Queen Street West, stop by this ever-evolving collection and snap a few pics for your Insta feed. Banksy hasn't blessed this spot (yet) but he did leave his mark around the corner on the wall of the Ocho Hotel (195 Spadina Ave.), which has since been painted over.

SLEEP
THE BEVERLY HOTEL
335 QUEEN ST. W • 416.493.2786

This 19-room minimalist boutique lodge in the middle of the Queen West bustle, originally opened in 2013, is now under new family-owned management, with a hip ground-floor shop featuring local finds and curated goods (think of it as a permanent pop-up). A bar, restaurant, and warm-weather rooftop patio ("The Nest") complete the out-of-room amenities and, in an interesting nod to efficiency, the lowest priced rooms (our choice), substitute rooftop light wells for windows. A snug fit at 150 square feet, crashing here with the bag + twigs was a bit of a bull-in-a-china-shop show, but all oddly comfortable.

BEER
LEAGUE
PICK
TIM THOMPSON

LISTEN
THE CAMERON HOUSE
408 QUEEN ST. W
416.703.0811

A family-run Queen West live music institution. Great artists, in a throwback atmosphere. And you can get lost just looking at the art on the walls. The owners care and it shows . . . and they are big Leafs fans too!

Rick Borg

COMMISSIONER,
THE DOWNTOWN
MEN'S HOCKEY
LEAGUE

For over 20 years, his league has been a haven for players of all caliber to hone their craft; anyone from accountants to lawyers to plumbers to musicians, such as Jim Cuddy of Blue Rodeo and Dave Bidini of Rheostatics.

EAT / DRINK

THE FOX

35 BAY ST.
416.869.3535
More of a local pub, directly across from the Toronto Islands. Spending the day and taking a walk by the lake to then cool off at this location would probably make for one of the best day outings you can get.

WAYNE GRETZKY'S [1]

99 BLUE JAYS WAY
416.348.0099
A hop, skip, and jump away from the Rogers Centre, for an after-event beverage. The atmosphere is laid back and caters to all ages. Definitely my first choice after a long, hard ball game!!

DAY TRIPS

Muskoka, day trips or week-long trips. Rice Lake, Simcoe, Couchaching, Holland River, Moon River Basin, and Sparrow Lake.

**INTERVIEW BY
ROB DEL MUNDO**

DMHL.CA

For those in the GTA looking to join a league, check out The Downtown Men's (and Women's) Hockey League—a great site to find a team, register a team, and to find available ice time at local rinks, in addition to contact info for available goalies. Most games are played at the following rinks:

PARAMOUNT ICE COMPLEX
1107 FINCH AVE. W
NORTH YORK

**BUCKINGHAM
DOWNSVIEW RINK**
57 CARL HALL RD.

THE RINX ARENA
65 ORFUS RD., NORTH YORK

UPPER CANADA COLLEGE
200 LONSDALE AVE.

DE LA SALLE ARENA
131 FARNHAM AVE.

BILL BOLTON ARENA
40 ROSSMORE RD.

VARSITY ARENA
275 BLOOR ST. W

MATTAMY ATHLETIC CENTRE
50 CARLTON ST.

GEORGE BELL ARENA
215 RYDING AVE.

**EAST YORK
MEMORIAL ARENA**
888 COSBURN AVE., EAST YORK

tor hub

SID SMITH RINK

777 CRAWFORD ST. • 416.392.7687

●●●●

Known for years as Christie Pits, this city-run neighborhood rink was recently renamed for the Toronto native who played for the Leafs from '46 to '58. During his playing days, he lived in the neighborhood, occasionally playing shinny with the locals after practicing with the pros, in what was clearly a simpler time. Typical of community rinks—wonders in their own right—sprinkled throughout the city, it's open every day from December to March for skating and shinny for various ages and skill levels. No skate rentals, but they do have lockers and basketball nets, just waiting for spring.

ROAD TRIP
PICK

ANDRE LEGASPI

BARBER / COFFEE
TOWN BARBER
1114 DUNDAS ST. W
416.399.3499
Coffee in the front,
haircut in the back.
After quickly gain-
ing popularity and
establishing itself as
a neighborhood main-
stay a few years into
its inception, Town
Barber expanded with
their recently opened
location on Dundas.
The original spot still
remains as popular as
ever, and the recent
addition of a coffee
bar at the front further
cements its laid-back
atmosphere. So, if you
need an expertly done
fade and an espresso,
you've found your
place.

EAT
CHANTECLER
1320 QUEEN ST. W
416.628.3586

Heading west on Queen Street, you can sense an
increase in shabby-chic, particularly as you enter
Parkdale, with small boutique spots like this gem.
With room for about 30 patrons, count your bless-
ings when you show up with no reservation and
you're offered a spot at the bar. You've been given the
best seat in the place.

VINYL
ROTATE THIS
186 OSSINGTON AVE.
416.504.8447

An obscene assortment of new and used records, organized alphabetically rather than by genre, making the wonderful accidents of crate digging all the more possible. An added bonus is that they're also an official ticket outlet for most of the major concert promoters in Toronto (cash only). They might even buy your old records, as long as you don't bring in anything by Poco (true story).

SHOP
BLUE TILE LOUNGE
822 DUNDAS ST. W
416.792.7171

Owned and operated by core members of the local skate scene going back two decades, this community-based shop features a premium selection of boards, apparel, and accessories.

MEMORIAL
GORD DOWNIE

While Drake, Nickleback, The Weeknd, Justin Bieber, and Arcade Fire all hail from the Great White North, no musical act is more profoundly, essentially Canadian than The Tragically Hip, whose frontman Gord Downie died of brain cancer in 2017. Though never gaining worldwide acclaim like those listed, it may well be because this alt blues garage band is so woven into the particular fabric of Canadian culture, that is, writing songs about hockey. Most notably the band's 1992 "Fifty-Mission Cap," which tells the story of Bill Barilko, the 24-year-old Toronto Maple Leafs defenseman who scored in overtime to clinch the Cup for the Leafs in 1951 only to vanish in a plane crash later that summer, his remains undiscovered for 11 years. Originally from Kingston, Ontario, the band got its first record deal after being spotted playing at the Horseshoe Tavern (page 29). Frontman Downie grew up a diehard Bruins fan, his godfather being the long-time Boston Bruins president Harry Sinden, and tended goal in his youth, inspiring the song "The Lonely End of the Rink." The band was known to play shinny when in the Toronto area, particularly outdoor games at Withrow Park. Upon Downie's death, the NHL Players' Association memorialized his connection to the sport: "The soundtrack of car rides to practices, bus trips to tournaments and dressing rooms across Canada. Hockey was a part of you and you will always be a part of hockey. Thank you, Gord Downie."

EAT / DRINK / LISTEN

THE DAKOTA TAVERN
249 OSSINGTON AVE. • 416.850.4579

Walking down the long flight of stairs to start your evening may seem a quaint embrace of local eccentricity, but the inevitable return back up from this basement honky tonk could bring with it a few moments of wobbly regret. This slice of Nashville in TO also offers a $30 CAD all-you-can-eat Sunday Bluegrass Brunch, but be prepared for a Benedict-less, firehouse pancake-style breakfast, all part of the charm with this fun, neighborhood haunt.

BEER LEAGUE PICKS
LIZ PEAD

EAT / DRINK

MADISON AVENUE PUB
14 MADISON AVE.
416.927.1722
Drinks with friends, great summer patio with big picnic tables.

DUKE OF YORK
39 PRINCE ARTHUR AVE.
416.964.2441
Cozy dinner with pub beers, watching the game or hanging on the patio.

BIG CROW
176 DUPONT ST.
647.748.3287
PASS THE RIBS.
Sneak down the side alley of Rose and Sons and you are there.

PLAY
TRINITY BELLWOODS RINK
GORE VALE AVE., SOUTH OF DUNDAS ST. W

City-run winter rink, with what they call "artificial ice," meaning man-made rather than naturally occurring (think pond). Kids' learn-to-skate programs are offered in addition to use by the community for pickup shinny games.

EAT / DRINK
ARCHIVE
909 DUNDAS ST. W
647.748.0909

Cozy wine and nibbles bar, offering an eclectic lineup of cheeses, while making a concerted effort to feature local Ontario grapes not named Don Cherry. For those not familiar with Mr. Cherry, frankly, we don't even know where to start. Fire up your browser and prepare to lose half a day, easy.

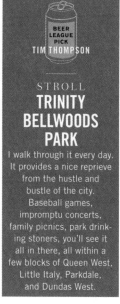

BEER
LEAGUE
PICK
TIM THOMPSON

STROLL
TRINITY BELLWOODS PARK

I walk through it every day. It provides a nice reprieve from the hustle and bustle of the city. Baseball games, impromptu concerts, family picnics, park drinking stoners, you'll see it all in there, all within a few blocks of Queen West, Little Italy, Parkdale, and Dundas West.

Auston Matthews
TORONTO MAPLE LEAFS
'16–PRESENT

The fate of Leaf world was thrust on this kid's shoulders from day one, and yes, he'll have some buds with him (Nylander, Marner, and, oh yeah, Tavares) but his task is singular and mighty: He has to win a Cup. Unless you've been living in a WiFi-less cave for the last few years, his story is not news—raised in the Arizona desert, joined the Swiss National League to play with grown-ups, four goals in his NHL debut (though a Leaf loss), and best rookie point total in Leafs 100-year existence. With a Mario-like combo of size and skill, he is one of a handful of current skaters who represent a generational shift in the game, making it seem as if everyone else is playing a previous iteration, if not standing still. His unique superpower: his shot release. His hands are so fast, he has a menu of options every time he tees it up. Following his four-goal debut, Ottawa's goalie, Fredrik Andersen, asked him to sign his stick. "Thanks FOUR making my first game memorable!" At least the kid's got a sense of humor, which he'll need because as this photo shows, when you're the chosen one, everyone's gunning for you (especially the guy chosen number two).

VINYL
JUNE RECORDS
662 COLLEGE ST. • 416.516.5863

We first heard about this vinyl boutique in journalist David Sax's *The Revenge of Analog: Real Things and Why They Matter*, an exploration into the renewed interest in the tangible, like records, board games, and . . . this book you're reading. In addition to its brick and mortar, June Records (ironically) also has a robust e-commerce outlet.

SOCKS
FLOORPLAY SOCKS
762 QUEEN ST. W • 416.504.7325

A few years back, the high magistrates of all things chic at *Vogue* magazine declared Queen West to be one of the globe's 15 coolest neighborhoods, and if you're still doubting and on the lookout for proof, we found it. Mike Babcock socks, complete with Leafs blue-and-white stripes. Another reminder to doubt Anna W. at your own peril.

BEER
LEAGUE
PICK
LIZ PEAD

SLEEP
THE GLADSTONE HOTEL

1214 QUEEN ST. W
416.531.4635

It's in the Queen West Art and Design District. I used to have a studio right around the corner, and now I go back to the Melody Bar to meet up with hockey peeps and for the karaoke. Also, the cafe has great local comfort food. The rooms are amazing! Designed by artists . . . and they usually have some kind of cool art exhibition going on in the common spaces.

This particular room was designed by Adam Berkowitz and George Simionopoulos.

COFFEE

THE NUGGET
761 DUNDAS ST. W

Something between a cafe and a pop-up, this converted garage run by the same crew behind neighboring Village Pizza offers a full menu of caffeinated (and decaf) options, including vegan coffee slushies, and a revolving splash of eye-catching and feet-stopping graffiti.

EAT
DEATH AND TAXES FREE HOUSE
1154 QUEEN ST. W • 416.533.5838

A relatively new (2017) pub, quirky and intimate, good for either an all-you-can-eat weekend brunch or a late-night bite, including their interesting take on pizza.

EAT / DRINK
HURRICANE'S ROADHOUSE
963 BLOOR ST. W • 416.531.7818

If you've been portrayed by Denzel Washington and inspired a Bob Dylan song, why shouldn't Ruben "The Hurricane" Carter be the namesake of a proud dive (sorry, Ruben) bar, known for its decent wings, fine patio, and exuberant Wednesday night karaoke.

TRUE NORTH HOCKEY
TRUENORTHHOCKEY.COM

This site organizes adult recreational hockey for men and women in the Toronto and Brampton, Ontario, areas—with an average winter league comprising about 420 teams, not players, *teams*. The majority of these register as a full team, and there is a player pool of free agents for the team reps and the league to recruit players. Games are played at the following rinks:

THE RINX ARENA
65 ORFUS RD., NORTH YORK

COCA-COLA COLISEUM
45 MANITOBA DR.

MATTAMY ATHLETIC CENTRE
50 CARLTON ST.

MASTERCARD CENTRE
400 KIPLING AVE.
ETOBICOKE

POWERADE CENTRE
7575 KENNEDY RD.
BRAMPTON

BEER LEAGUE PICK LIZ PEAD

PLAY
DUFFERIN GROVE
875 DUFFERIN ST.
Close to TTC just south of Bloor-Danforth line at Dufferin. The cafe features coffee, hot chocolate, home baking, and even a wood-fired pizza oven! Grab your skates, gloves, and helmet and find a spot on the bench.

SLEEP / EAT / DRINK
THE DRAKE HOTEL
1150 QUEEN ST. W • 416.531.5042

Calm down, it's not *his* hotel, but it probably wasn't the worst thing when only a few years after their 2004 opening, young Aubrey arrived to give both this place and this town an instant cred injection. Now a beehive of the creative set, with 19 uniquely designed rooms, from 150-square-foot Crash Pad to 385-square-foot XL Suite. And in addition to a restaurant, the Sky Yard rooftop bar and Drake Underground (the hotel's lounge and performance space), across the street you'll find Drake General Store, a hotel gift / museum shop with a carefully curated mix of wares from local artisans and those of like minds from abroad.

EAT / DRINK
THE DOCK ELLIS
1280 DUNDAS ST. W • 416.792.8472

An unpretenious sports bar, with imaginative pub food and solid draught selection along with shuffleboard, pool, foosball, and darts. Named for (but with no connection to) the MLBer who in 1970 pitched a no-hitter while on LSD, later revealing "sometimes I saw the catcher, sometimes I didn't." According to hardball lore, Ellis took the acid not realizing what day it was and upon being reminded he was scheduled to pitch, made his way to the stadium.

VINYL

KOPS RECORDS

592 BLOOR ST. W • 647.352.8523

The original location on Queen Street West is the city's oldest independent record business, dating back to 1976. This location opened in 2015, with a warehouse section in the back where they keep their 75,000 overstock of LPs. We don't expect you to haul your crates up to Toronto (because you've already brought your gear) but if you are selling, make an appointment to have them size up your collection, which they can do in a few minutes.

1

Paul Hendrick

VETERAN
BROADCASTER

To a legion of viewers on Leafs TV, he's the host of the pregame and postgame panels. Indeed, veteran broadcaster Paul Hendrick has paid his dues, from his humble beginnings at CKCY in Sault Ste. Marie, then to CHCH in Hamilton where the opportunity to join the Leafs broadcasts materialized.

The rest, as they say, is history.

"It's a career that's pushing on 40 years and two decades with the Toronto Maple Leafs," says the affable man nicknamed Henny. His research is impeccable as he is often tasked with interviewing players for game-day features. As such, Hendrick can recall a skater's favorite hobby, or food, or even point out his parents in the crowd—on a first-name basis of course—with a photographic memory.

"Nothing is more sat-

**INTERVIEW BY
ROB DEL MUNDO**

isfying to me than getting down and peeling the onion," Hendrick says. "I'm talking about digging deep into a player's past."

The quick-witted Hendrick will forever be known to longtime viewers for his Leafs pregame teasers that blended rhymes, puns, and alliteration, as if the introduction was a song jingle. Example: If Jonas Hoglund was expected to step up his game in the absence of an injured Mats Sundin, then Hendrick would call for the Leafs to "put the onus on Jonas." Another favorite was assembled when Anaheim paid a visit, and

was still performing strongly despite missing future Hall of Famers Paul Kariya and Teemu Selanne: "there's no lack of quack in the Duck attack."

"It was an appetizer for the main entrée," Hendrick recalls of the popular game teases.

Away from the ACC, he has another home rink. On Tuesday mornings, for 10 months of the year, Henny skates with his longtime cronies at a rink in Parkdale. The ritual among close friends has extended into two decades. "I'm 60, and we've been playing for what seems like forever."

2

PLAY
MCCORMICK ARENA
179 BROCK AVE.
416.392.0647

EAT
BAR RAVAL[1]
505 COLLEGE ST.
647.344.8001
I love Spanish food, especially tapas; if you do too, well you'll revel in Raval.

MAMMA MARTINO'S
624 THE QUEENSWAY
ETOBICOKE
416.251.3337
Go hungry and order the chicken parm with spaghetti bolognese as the side; a glass of medicinal house rouge helps too!

THE TREMONT CAFE
80 SIMCOE ST., COLLINGWOOD
705.293.6000

DRINK / BARBER
ROD, GUN AND BARBERS[2]
2877 DUNDAS ST. W
647.350.6446
You can't beat the relaxed ambience sipping on a beverage in a fishing lodge/barbershop environment in the midst of The Junction.

SHOP
JEROME'S MENSWEAR
2603 YONGE ST.
416.489.2494

tor hub
HOCKEY HALL OF FAME
30 YONGE ST.
416.360.7765

●●●

Containing the single greatest collection of hockey artifacts on the planet, this place is a shrine to which you simply must make a pilgrimage. While most of the exhibits sit quietly behind glass: gloves, sticks, skates, jerseys (actually sweaters, when they were actual sweaters), some do not, like the full replica of the Canadians locker room from the old Forum. For the true fan, the experience here borders on the religious. You'll read the placard accompanying the stick Gretzky used to score his record 92nd goal in 1982 and you'll find yourself staring at it, a hockey stick, unable to believe that you're in its presence. Similarly, you'll come upon a puck, identical to every other puck you've ever seen, and it turns out to be the one Sidney Crosby shot in over-time to win the Olympic gold medal in 2010. That puck.

EAT / DRINK
THE BOTTOM LINE
22 FRONT ST. W • 416.362.7585

His entire career as an NHL goalie: one game.
Did he win? How many goals did he let in? Save
percentage? Irrelevant. Whether Wayne Cowley
reached the pinnacle for one game or a thousand
simply doesn't matter. And if you stop by his iconic
bar steps away from the Hockey Hall of Fame and
if you ask nicely, he'll pull up a chair and tell you
some stories—of which he has many. And he's not
the only one. This spot is known for the ex-pros
who stop by and tell their tales. "We keep a copy
of 'The Hockey Bible,' he says, showing us a large,
worn copy of the NHL official stats for every player.
"Always on hand to settle all the arguments, with
facts only the book could confirm." We sneaked
a look and, okay, he didn't win and he let in three
goals. But at least he's got the story . . . and the bar.

BEER
LEAGUE
PICK
TIM THOMPSON

EAT / DRINK
THE BEER BISTRO
18 KING ST. E
416.861.9872
An extensive beer list and
great food . . . quite possibly the most unique and
best chicken wings I've
ever had.

CAFFEINE
DINEEN COFFEE CO.
140 YONGE ST.
416.900.0949

An elegant Viennese cafe with floor-to-ceiling windows morphs into a hangout for those in search of WiFi and cortados, all on the ground floor of the historic Dineen Building, originally built in 1897. With a menu full of fine coffee, baked goods, sandwiches, and salads, this people-watching corner spot has two other locations: Dineen Outpost at 1042 Gerrard Street East and Dineen Commerce Court at 199 Bay Street.

MY PICKS
David Amber
HOCKEY NIGHT IN CANADA
Grew up playing in the GTHL but reality hit hard when he tried out for his McGill University team, unsuccessfully, allowing for more time concentrating on his journalism degree.

PLAY
UCC / WILLIAM WILDER ARENA
200 LONSDALE RD.
416.488.1125

RESOURCE
20SKATERS.COM
Great site that helps pickup game organizers.

GEAR
MAJER HOCKEY
4610 DUFFERIN ST., NORTH YORK • 416.736.7444

SLEEP
SHANGRI-LA HOTEL
188 UNIVERSITY AVE.
647.788.8888

CAFFEINE
DINEEN COFFEE CO.
SEE LEFT
A buddy of mine, Dave Fortier, opened this place, kind of the anti-Starbucks.

SHOP
SPIRIT OF HOCKEY
30 YONGE ST.
416.360.7735 EXT. 6

The gift shop for the Hockey Hall of Fame, located inside Brookfield Place, has every team represented, at every price level. Serious fans will become intoxicated by the volume. (US shoppers: Don't forget to check the exchange rate before entering to calm any buyer's guilt in advance.)

ANDRE LEGASPI

SLEEP
THE STRATHCONA HOTEL
60 YORK ST.
416.363.3321

You won't find a better home base than this spot. Reasonably priced, it also has a full-fledged pub popular with pregamers.

EAT / DRINK
AMSTERDAM BICYCLE CLUB
54 THE ESPLANADE
416.864.9996

On The Esplanade, what some consider the best patio street in the city (and this city is patio-heavy), this spot, with no evident connection to Amsterdam or cycling, features live music, stand-up, and "Opera pub night" on the first Thursday of every month, so plan ahead. You know how opera crowds can be.

BEER LEAGUE PICKS
LIZ PEAD

LISTEN
MASSEY HALL
178 VICTORIA ST.
416.872.4255

My all-time fave concert venue. The sound is great, the ambiance lovely. The full package. And the seats are comfortable enough for giant hockey players, although I hear they are going to fix the ol' gal up a bit.

TATTOO
SUGOI TATTOO
295 QUEEN ST. E

Chris Wellard did my ink, and it was one of the best pieces of art I ever got.

TEETH
QUEEN ST. DENTAL CARE
1 QUEEN ST. E
416-364-6464

Once upon a time, I was going to the Art Gallery of Ontario and my bicycle followed the streetcar tracks . . . they fixed my head.

EAT
LOADED PIEROGI
9 1/2 CHURCH ST. • 647.344.0088

A bit of hockey cuisine lore: When Marian Hossa wins a Stanley Cup, he brings it home to Slovakia, pulls up a chair, and dines on pierogis, little miracles often called the perfect food—straight from the Cup. At this place, which has five locations in the city, choose your pierogi, then your topping, then your vodka.

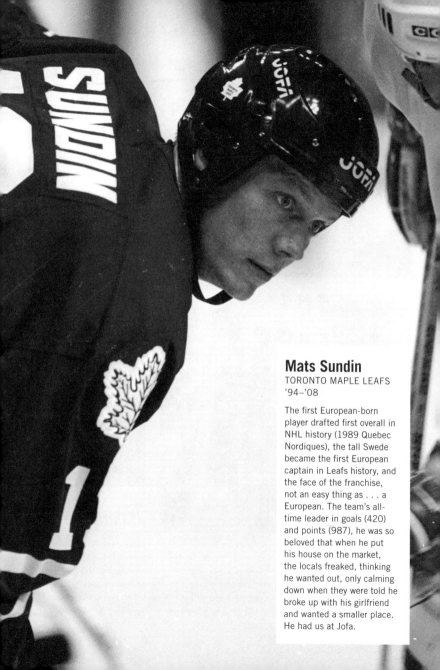

Mats Sundin
TORONTO MAPLE LEAFS
'94–'08

The first European-born
player drafted first overall in
NHL history (1989 Quebec
Nordiques), the tall Swede
became the first European
captain in Leafs history, and
the face of the franchise,
not an easy thing as . . . a
European. The team's all-
time leader in goals (420)
and points (987), he was so
beloved that when he put
his house on the market,
the locals freaked, thinking
he wanted out, only calming
down when they were told he
broke up with his girlfriend
and wanted a smaller place.
He had us at Jofa.

ROAD TRIP PICK

ANDRE LEGASPI

DRINK
SPEAKEASY 21
21 ADELAIDE ST. W
416.601.0210

Getting a beer at one of the bars in this neighborhood can involve swimming through a sea of Tucker or Kadri jerseys before getting the bartender's attention. To avoid the aggravation, non-Leaf fans can head to this spot, which is usually a happy hour or lunch spot for corporate types in the afternoon. The gastropub has a tasty roster of cocktails and the refined grub is a step up from the usual. Bonus points for not having to face a single elbow or blindside hit to get a drink.

EAT
PLANTA BURGER
4 TEMPERANCE ST.
647.348.7000

Hip eatery featuring a 100-percent plant-based menu, healthy for both the body and the planet. Head 20 minutes north, and you'll arrive at their second location, Planta Toronto (1221 Bay Street).

SHOP
HAVEN
190 RICHMOND ST. E, FLOOR 2
416.901.1195

Featuring sought-after sneakers and high-end streetwear in a clean, sparse environment.

SHOP
PATH

Relative to the rest of Canada, you'll find that a Toronto winter is a mild one, temperature-wise. Still, assume the following for the three-month stretch: it'll be consistently five degrees below freezing; a general discomfort coming from the wind off Lake Ontario; and an ever-present grey dampness. Solution: stay inside, hence PATH. There are 1,200 stores, along with restaurants, parking garages, and subway lines, all connected by the largest under-ground pedestrian system in North America. Another solution: step into one of the 957 bars in the city.

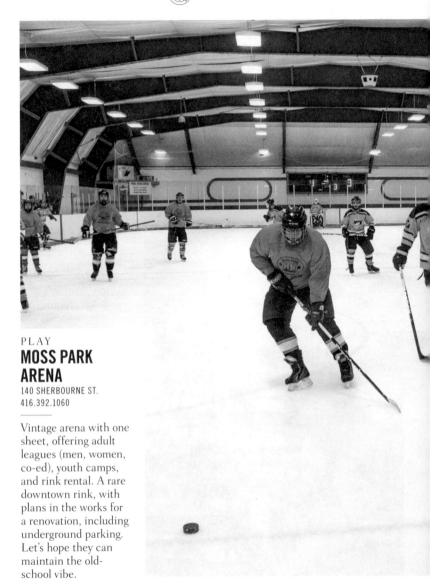
PLAY
MOSS PARK ARENA
140 SHERBOURNE ST.
416.392.1060

Vintage arena with one sheet, offering adult leagues (men, women, co-ed), youth camps, and rink rental. A rare downtown rink, with plans in the works for a renovation, including underground parking. Let's hope they can maintain the old-school vibe.

MY PICKS

Phil Pritchard

CUP HANDLER,
HOCKEY HALL OF
FAME

For nearly three decades, Phil Pritchard has been present for the final, and most memorable, game of the NHL season. Along with Craig Campbell, Pritchard has the enviable task of carrying hockey's holy grail—handled with white gloves, of course—to center ice, where the Cup is received by the NHL commissioner, and then the ecstatic captain of the winning team.

Pritchard's official title is Vice President, Resource Centre and Curator at the Hockey Hall of Fame; however he is informally known as simply "the keeper of the Cup." He describes the feeling of the waning moments of any Cup-clinching game as one of nervousness and excitement.

"As it winds down you can feel the excitement not only from the

INTERVIEW BY
ROB DEL MUNDO

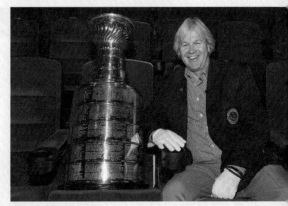

fans and the team that's about to win it, but also the staff that are working behind the scenes to make it all happen," Pritchard says.

"It's not just the sense of excitement for everybody, but the sense of relief from the captain that they've finally done it, that they've achieved their ultimate business goal in capturing the Cup."

When he's not touring from city to city, or from country to country as mandated by the off-season tour during which every member of the winning team gets his day with Lord Stanley, Pritchard oversees the displays at the Hockey Hall of Fame and acquires artifacts for the collection.

Hockey historians are well-versed in the anecdotes of the Stanley Cup's escapades. The trophy has been drop-kicked in the Rideau Canal. It has been inadvertently left on a street corner.

From his years of global travel, Pritchard has a myriad of tales, all witnessed from his rare, firsthand perspective.

"Each one of the stories are unique in their own way," he says, "whether it's Anze Kopitar taking it to Slovenia for the first time, or Teemu Selanne going back to Finland and having a sauna party with his family and friends, or Kris Letang taking it up in northern Quebec to a cottage and having a band playing out on the front deck of his pool."

Like most Canadian kids, Pritchard grew up wanting to win the Stanley Cup as a player. The on-ice career didn't pan out, but his current job is a perfect substitute for those dreams.

Splitting time at the Master-Card Centre at the Hockey Hall of Fame archives and downtown Toronto at the Hockey Hall of Fame, I often try to get out to some local, small establishments in and around the archives.

EAT
IL PAESANO'S
396 BROWN'S LINE, ETOBICOKE
416.251.7080
Great pizza.

SPOON AND FORK
1233 THE QUEENSWAY #24
ETOBICOKE
416.201.8688
Always a work favorite, as we often do group outings there from the office.

THE CANTEEN AT THE MASTERCARD CENTRE
400 KIPLING AVE, ETOBICOKE
416.251.5219
When we want great food that is easily accessible and has a

great cook with a great selection, just ask any high school kid who comes from blocks away to get lunch every day.

THAI ISLAND
181 BAY ST.
416.850.0987
When I'm downtown at the Hockey Hall of Fame, I love the noodles here.

EAT / DRINK
BLUE GOOSE TAVERN [1]
1 BLUE GOOSE ST.
ETOBICOKE
416.255.2442
Pretty hard to beat the old-style bar atmosphere, where cash is still king and the beer is always cold.

THE BOTTOM LINE
22 FRONT ST. W
416.362.7585
At night, everyone goes for a beer right around the corner from the Hockey Hall of Fame. Wayne Cowley, the owner, always finds a spot for our staff.

DAY TRIPS
& BEYOND
Being on the west side in Burlington, our travels often take us to Lake Huron or Lake Erie for camping and fish frys. The best perch in the world is from Lake Erie.

SHOUT OUT
BRONTE FISH & CHIPS
2313 LAKESHORE RD. W,
OAKVILLE
905.827.1644
This place has been owned by my wife's family for 50 years. A community favorite with the best fish & chips in

1

the world. I think I can say that fairly, as traveling all across this great country and to more than 24 countries for my job I get the chance to try all different foods. Great fish & chips up in Yellowknife, Northwest Territories as well, but none as good as the family business.

tor hub

ST. MICHAEL'S COLLEGE SCHOOL ARENA

1515 BATHURST ST., YORK
416.653.3180

Maybe it's the water in the drinking fountains at this all-boys Catholic school, but they have a habit of sending players to the NHL, going back over a hundred years, such as Turk Broda, Dick Duff, Ted Lindsay, Tim Horton, Red Kelly, Dave Keon, Frank Mahovlich, Cesare Maniago, Gerry Cheevers, Rod Seiling, Peter Budaj, Casey Cizikas, Cal Clutterbuck, Kevin Klein, Zac Rinaldo, Devante Smith-Pelly . . . we could go on but we're almost out of space. The skaters pictured here are 2004s, so check back in about five years and see who made it, because odds are, someone did.

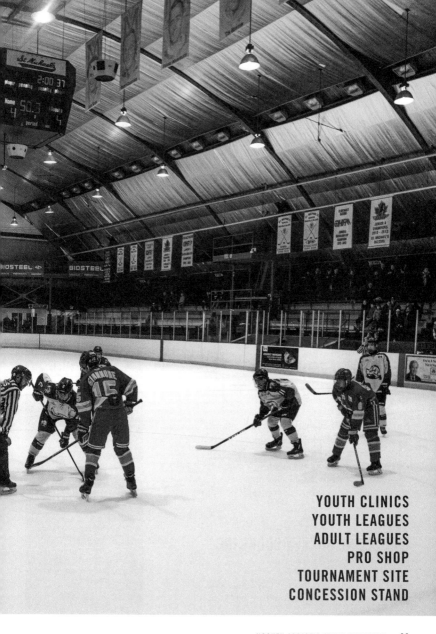

YOUTH CLINICS
YOUTH LEAGUES
ADULT LEAGUES
PRO SHOP
TOURNAMENT SITE
CONCESSION STAND

EAT
STARVING ARTIST
1078 ST. CLAIR AVE. W
416.901.7479

Large, loud, and lively cash-only neighborhood favorite serving all-day, waffle-based fare, perfect for the carb-obsessed crowd. In addition, this spot (and its three additional Toronto locations) supports local artists with new work displayed every six weeks, though we seriously doubt those showcased could possibly be starving given the menu.

SOCKS
MODELLINE HOCKEY SOCKS INC.
660 VAUGHAN RD., YORK • 416.652.3712

Family-run business founded by Grandpa Gino in 1965 manufactures and sells one product: knit hockey socks.

BEER
LEAGUE
PICKS
LIZ PEAD

EAT / DRINK
BAR BEGONIA
252 DUPONT ST.
647.352.3337
A little farther down Dupont, just before Spadina. More french nibbles and cocktails.

EAT / DRINK
MADAME BOEUF AND FLEA
252 DUPONT ST.
647.352.3337
In the backyard of Begonia, serving up some pretty serious BBQ if the nibbles need some assistance.

GEAR
AVENUE ROAD SPORTS
1775 AVENUE RD.
NORTH YORK
416.784.1500

While stocking equipment for lacrosse, soccer, and baseball, their specialty is hockey, with expert skate and equipment fitting, skate profiling, and equipment repair and sanitizing. If only our own gear was as organized as the stuff in this place.

SWEATERS, ETC.
COOLHOCKEY
72 KINCORT ST., YORK
888.454.9190

Team jerseys and apparel, in addition to customizing officially licensed NHL jerseys.

Dave Keon
TORONTO MAPLE LEAFS
'60–'75

As part of their centennial celebration in 2016, the Leafs' organization settled the debate and selected the greatest player in team history. The speedy 5'9", 165 lb, two-way center who brought home four Cups— three consecutively—Keon became estranged from the franchise following a bitter breakup with then-owner, the notorious curmudgeon, Harold Ballard. The brouhaha was the result of, what else, a nasty contract dispute, which resulted in Keon being unable to sign with another NHL team, exiling him to the WHA. He eventually made his return to the NHL with the awesomely logo'd Hartford Whalers when the two leagues merged in 1979, though, oddly, the Leafs still owned Keon's NHL rights, giving Ballard one more chance to stick it to Keon. The NY Islanders, on the cusp of greatness, wanted a veteran checking center in their young lineup but Ballard's demand for unrealistic compensation killed the deal, leading the Isles to acquire Butch Goring. The rest is history or, in Keon's case, a justified cold shoulder to the franchise, which took decades to soothe.

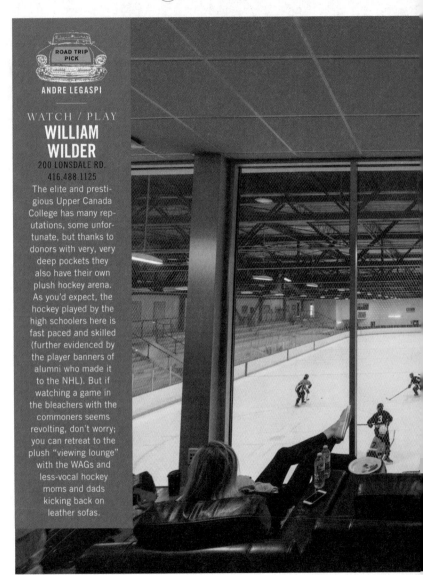

ROAD TRIP PICK

ANDRE LEGASPI

WATCH / PLAY
WILLIAM WILDER

200 LONSDALE RD.
416.488.1125

The elite and prestigious Upper Canada College has many reputations, some unfortunate, but thanks to donors with very, very deep pockets they also have their own plush hockey arena. As you'd expect, the hockey played by the high schoolers here is fast paced and skilled (further evidenced by the player banners of alumni who made it to the NHL). But if watching a game in the bleachers with the commoners seems revolting, don't worry; you can retreat to the plush "viewing lounge" with the WAGs and less-vocal hockey moms and dads kicking back on leather sofas.

tor hub

TORONTO HOCKEY REPAIR

1592 BLOOR ST. W
416.533.1791

The GTA has so many hockey shops, they can easily be divided into categories; mom & pop, franchise, big box, and rink pro shops. Welcome to a shining example of a mom & pop—cramped and a bit crazy, but a true throwback, like a diner that knows it has the best burger in town. Pretty much every skater we asked mentioned this mecca as a go-to, whether for equipment or a sharpening. Don't be confused by the name, they carry everything (new and used) and fix everything else. You can even send them busted equipment and they'll stitch it up and send it back. Adjacent to the main store is Goalie Heaven, their outlet dedicated to serving the unique requirements of goalies (and we all agree to putting tenders in their own room). Not promising you'll run into ex-Leaf Phil Kessel, but rumor has it he's had some work done here. Then again, you might have a better chance of running into him at the diner.

DRINK
SHAKEY'S
2255 BLOOR ST. W
416.767.0608

This establishment was originally opened by Mike "Shakey" Walton, St. Michael's alumnus and later a center for the Maple Leafs '67 Cup winners (the following year becoming the team's leading scorer). His inclusion into Toronto hockey royalty was sealed with his marriage to Conn Smythe's granddaughter, Candace. The nickname, a hand-me-down from his father whose signature move was a shake of the head to fake out an opponent.

BEER
LEAGUE
PICK
LIZ PEAD

POOL
SHOXS
BILLIARDS
LOUNGE
2827 DUNDAS ST. W.
416.762.7097
Pub grub, draft beers, and pool. Good hangout after hockey at George Bell Arena.

ROAD TRIP PICK

ANDRE LEGASPI

PLAY
GEORGE BELL ARENA

215 RYDING AVE.
416.392.0377

What was once the home rink of the Ryerson Rams and the practice arena of the Maple Leafs, George Bell is now home to a house league for kids (George Bell Titans), women's leagues, and various tournaments. But ask anyone with any knowledge of the arena and they'll be quick to mention the great Gordie Howe, who supposedly set foot on their ice.

SWEATERS
BIG STICK
2238 DUNDAS ST. W
416.934.0978

Interesting name for a custom jersey company. Ordering is completed online (bigstick.ca), with a showroom to touch some samples. Produced locally with worldwide distribution.

DRINK
ROUND THE HORN
331 RONCESVALLES AVE.
416.785.2123

Jenga, Scrabble, hot dogs, Nintendo, pinball, free candy: This place would be a go-to even without the alcohol, which they do have, specializing in tall cans of local craft beer.

MY PICKS

Christine Simpson
VETERAN BROADCASTER
The first in-arena host for the Toronto Maple Leafs, and best known for her in-depth features presented on *Hockey Night in Canada*, Simpson worked as marketing manager at the Hockey Hall of Fame before starting her journalism career.

ART
ART GALLERY OF ONTARIO
317 DUNDAS ST. W
416.979.6648
Always worth a visit as well as lunch at their restaurant, Frank.

CULTURE
THE HOCKEY HALL OF FAME
30 YONGE ST. • 416.360.7765
A must-see and not just for hockey fans. I worked there for five years so it always holds a special place in my heart.

WORKOUT
BARRE BEAUTIFUL
2156 YONGE ST. • 647.748.2156
My daily workout is doing barre classes at this studio.

HAIR
FIORIO
136 CUMBERLAND ST.
416.964.5737
Favorite hair salon is in Yorkville. The best!

EAT
FIVE DOORS NORTH
2088 YONGE ST. • 416.480.6234
Fave neighborhood restaurant.

KASA MOTO
115 YORKVILLE AVE.
647.348.7000
A rooftop for great sushi in the summertime.

MONTECITO
299 ADELAIDE ST. W
416.599.0299
Great dinner and brunch.

SOTTO VOCE
595 COLLEGE ST.
416.536.4564
Outdoor patios in Little Italy, especially at this spot with great food and a good vibe.

MUSIC
BUDWEISER STAGE
909 LAKE SHORE BLVD. W
416.260.5600
Concerts here are the perfect way to spend a summer night by Lake Ontario.

INTERVIEW BY ROB DEL MUNDO

DRINK
NICKEL 9 DISTILLERY
90 CAWTHRA AVE. • 647.341.5959

In 1904, an ordinance was passed outlawing the production or sale of alcohol in the Junction, a neighborhood with a rich history of drunken unruliness. For nearly a century, the locals ventured elsewhere in search of their sauce but, thankfully, alcohol returned to the area in 2000, leading to an influx of a new generation of brewers, distillers, and patrons. Fast forward to 2017 and the arrival of Nickel 9 Distillery whose founders' goal was to use only locally sourced ingredients in the production of their spirits. While having years of critical distilling experience, they also had some ice time: Harris grew up playing on the pond while Chris played Junior C. With an on-site retail store and sample bar, this craft distillery offers tours that feature cocktail samples, including their Northern Temple vodka (made from Ontario apples), and the option to fill your own bottle.

ROAD TRIP PICK

ANDRE LEGASPI

AXE
THROWING
BAD AXE
THROWING
346 RYDING AVE. #201K
416.604.4815

The pseudo-outdoorsy pastime of axe throwing became available to Torontonians in 2015, when throwing darts suddenly became boring to millennials and Bad Axe Throwing set up shop in the Junction neighborhood, giving this distressed generation a place to release their existential frustration by hurling heavy axes at innocent wooden targets.

Borje Salming
Toronto Maple Leafs
'73–'89

The first non-royal Swede referred to as "The King" was a guy signed as an undrafted European and thrown on the ice into the teeth of the NHL, mid-70s edition. When scout and future GM Gerry McNamara made the trans-Atlantic trip to check out winger Inge Hammarstrom (who would also join the Leafs), he wound up bringing home raves for a player who would change the game, making the collective mouth water for a team from Broad Street, who saw some fresh 22-year-old meat for dinner. Problem was, this skinny kid wasn't on the menu. Swedes (and all foreigners) were considered skilled but soft until this tall, smooth D-man showed up, taking beatings and coming back for more, forging a path for the hoard of Euros who followed. A possible key to this guy's resilience—growing up 90 miles *north* of the Arctic Circle. A few stats: 16 seasons; highest scoring defenseman in Leafs history (and all-time assist leader); for a four-year stretch, practically a point-a-game player (*as a defenseman*); first Swede in the HHOF; all the while engaging in only a handful of fights. Sure, Philly would win their first Cup the year Salming enters the league, perfecting the craft of hooliganism, but he got his revenge, launching an underwear line and three cookbooks, all with the dead-eye stare.

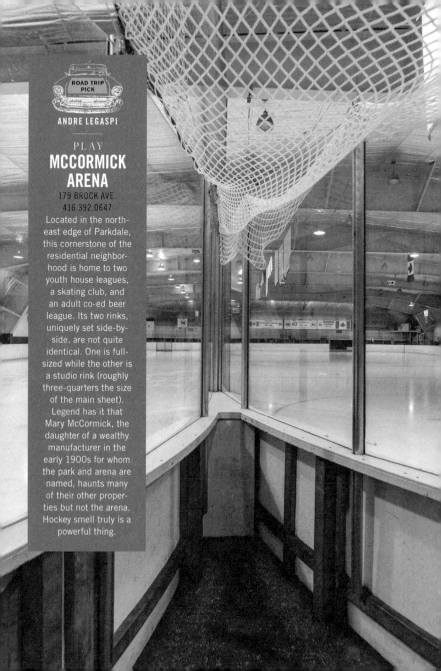

ANDRE LEGASPI

PLAY

MCCORMICK ARENA

179 BROCK AVE.
416.392.0647

Located in the north-
east edge of Parkdale,
this cornerstone of the
residential neighbor-
hood is home to two
youth house leagues,
a skating club, and
an adult co-ed beer
league. Its two rinks,
uniquely set side-by-
side, are not quite
identical. One is full-
sized while the other is
a studio rink (roughly
three-quarters the size
of the main sheet).

Legend has it that
Mary McCormick, the
daughter of a wealthy
manufacturer in the
early 1900s for whom
the park and arena are
named, haunts many
of their other proper-
ties but not the arena.
Hockey smell truly is a
powerful thing.

1

| MY PICKS |

Natasha Staniszewski

SPORTSCENTRE ANCHOR

Putting journalistic integrity aside, the staff at the Scarborough-based studios of TSN (Canada's version of ESPN) gets amped when a Toronto team enjoys success.

"I was at work for Auston Matthews' first game, when he scored four goals," recalls Staniszewski. "There was a buzz in the newsroom. A huge moment."

The Edmonton native never played hockey as a youngster, excelling instead at basketball and volleyball. To get outside her comfort zone and to get in some exercise, she joined a floor hockey team at the Toronto Sport and Social Club (see page 159).

"It was a co-ed team, and they're always looking for girls, so they were happy to have me. I thought it would be fun to play on a team again," she remembers.

Proud of her Polish heritage, Staniszewski occasionally partakes in a pierogi-based meal in the city's Little Poland neighborhood, and, in another nod to her lineage, she cites Wojtek Wolski as her favorite player from that country. "I just love his name, it rolls off the tongue," she says.

And as for her own last name?

"I feel bad for my co-anchors who have to learn how to pronounce it. It's really not that bad but it's intimidating at first."

EAT

CAFE POLONEZ [1]

195 RONCESVALLES AVE.
416.532.8432
I've been there for pierogis. It reminds me of when my Edmonton grandma would make them for me all the time.

SCHOOL

70 FRASER AVE.
416.588.0005
It's one of my favorite places for brunch.

GOLF

ISLINGTON GOLF CLUB

45 RIVERBANK DR., ETOBICOKE
416.231.1114

INTERVIEW BY ROB DEL MUNDO

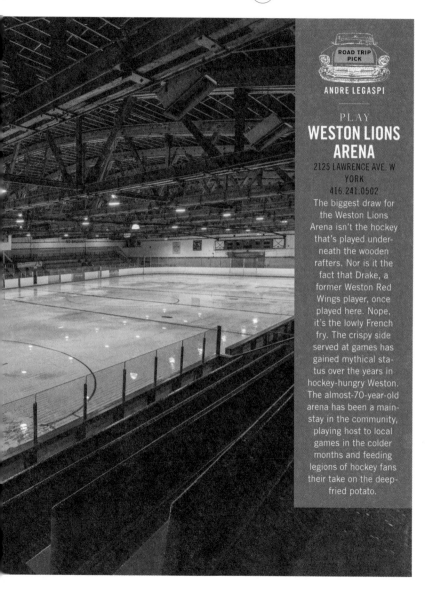

ROAD TRIP
PICK

ANDRE LEGASPI

PLAY

WESTON LIONS ARENA

2125 LAWRENCE AVE. W
YORK
416.241.0502

The biggest draw for the Weston Lions Arena isn't the hockey that's played underneath the wooden rafters. Nor is it the fact that Drake, a former Weston Red Wings player, once played here. Nope, it's the lowly French fry. The crispy side served at games has gained mythical status over the years in hockey-hungry Weston. The almost-70-year-old arena has been a mainstay in the community, playing host to local games in the colder months and feeding legions of hockey fans their take on the deep-fried potato.

MY PICKS

Dave Bidini

GUITARIST,
RHEOSTATICS;
AUTHOR;
EDITOR *WEST END
PHOENIX*

It's Saturday night and Dave Bidini is missing a weekly beer league game, with good reason. He has swapped his hockey stick for a guitar, and is on stage at Toronto's legendary Horseshoe Tavern, finger-picking his way through a set along with his longtime bandmates, Rheostatics.

"Music and hockey are both physically and intellectually engaging and stimulating," Bidini says. "As long as you go through life, you just want to try to maintain the things that make you happy."

Indeed Bidini has embarked on several projects aside from Rheostatics. His published books include *The Hockey Nomad*, *Writing Gordon Lightfoot*, and *Baseballisimo*. In the summer of 2017, Bidini founded *West End Phoenix*, a Toronto nonprofit, community-based newspaper.

Amidst all the organized chaos, Bidini never strays far from the rink. He has spent the better part of a decade playing as a goalie with a women's team. And although he participates regularly in a few midweek skates, nothing matches the feeling of donning the sweater of his longtime squad, the Morningstars.

The team jersey that features a white star on a red background is depicted on the cover of Bidini's book *The Best Game You Can Name*, and several pages of the vol-

INTERVIEW BY ROB DEL MUNDO

PLAY
GEORGE BELL ARENA
215 RYDING AVE.
416.392.0377

MCCORMICK ARENA
179 BROCK AVE.
416.392.0647

BILL BOLTON ARENA
40 ROSSMORE RD.
416.392.0088

WALLACE EMERSON RINK ARENA
1260 DUFFERIN ST.
416.392.0911

GEAR
TORONTO HOCKEY REPAIR
1592 BLOOR ST. W
416.533.1791

ume are devoted to chronicling the Morningstars' trials and tribulations.

"It's been 23 years for us," Bidini said of his Saturday-night squad. "We've traveled together, lost together, and we've maintained this very strong bond among men. It's lovely how the team has main-

MUSIC VENUES
THE MOD CLUB
722 COLLEGE ST.
416.588.4663

CASTRO'S LOUNGE
2116 QUEEN ST. E
416.699.8272

HORSESHOE TAVERN
370 QUEEN ST. W
416.598.4226

THE BURDOCK
1184 BLOOR ST. W
416.546.4033

VINYL
KOPP'S ON QUEEN STREET
229 QUEEN ST. W
416.593.8523

SOUNDSCAPES
572 COLLEGE ST.
416.537.1620

RANSACK THE UNIVERSE
1207 BLOOR ST. W
647.703.6675

tained an important presence in our lives. Hockey is one of the glues that allows us to stay together."

The Morningstars will forgive him for missing the skate on the occasion of

EAT / DRINK
THE SKYLINE
1426 QUEEN ST. W
416.536.3682

THE EMERSON
1279 BLOOR ST. W
416.532.1717

ENOTECHA SOCIALE
1288 DUNDAS ST. W
416.534.1200

THE BROCKTON HAUNT
1150 COLLEGE ST.
647.340.5743

LA BANANE
227 OSSINGTON AVE.
416.551.6263

JUNCTION CRAFT BREWERY
150 SYMES RD.
416.766.1616

HONEST WEIGHT
2766 DUNDAS ST. W
416.604.9992

Rheostatics' fourth concert at the Horseshoe in as many nights. For Bidini, wailing away on a six-string is just as satisfying as firing a puck into the top shelf.

"I never put away my toys," he says.

tor hub
MATTAMY
ATHLETIC CENTRE
50 CARLTON ST.

●●●●

You've made your way to the corner of Carlton and Church in search of a shrine, but if you're not paying attention, you'll think you've made a mistake. What you notice first is a supermarket on the corner (see page 95), then the building itself—maybe it's a post office or some mid-level government agency—then finally the marquee, with typography from another era. Soon enough you're imagining the whole block in black and white, the street packed with oversized cars with rounded tops and bloated fenders. Completed in just over five months (think about that the next time you're re-doing your kitchen), Maple Leaf Gardens was home to the NHL franchise from '31 to '99, when they moved to the Air Canada Centre (recently re-named the Scotiabank Arena). Now the Mattamy Athletic Centre, Ryerson University's sports complex includes an NHL-sized rink—home ice to the Ryerson Rams—and is also available for shinny games, adult league, and tournament rental.

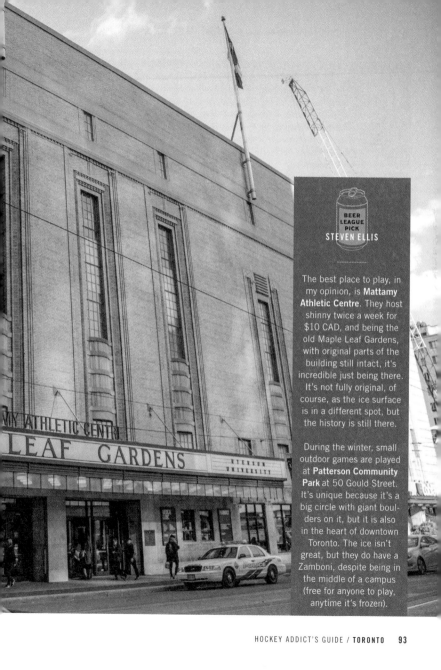

BEER
LEAGUE
PICK
STEVEN ELLIS

The best place to play, in my opinion, is **Mattamy Athletic Centre**. They host shinny twice a week for $10 CAD, and being the old Maple Leaf Gardens, with original parts of the building still intact, it's incredible just being there. It's not fully original, of course, as the ice surface is in a different spot, but the history is still there.

During the winter, small outdoor games are played at **Patterson Community Park** at 50 Gould Street. It's unique because it's a big circle with giant boulders on it, but it is also in the heart of downtown Toronto. The ice isn't great, but they do have a Zamboni, despite being in the middle of a campus (free for anyone to play, anytime it's frozen).

ROAD TRIP PICK

ANDRE LEGASPI

KICKS
CAPSULE
69 YORKVILLE AVE. #104
647.748.1169
The Yorkville section of Toronto conveniently squeezes all the high-end boutiques in the span of a few blocks. In the middle of it all is Capsule, a sneaker-head's paradise. Its walls are stocked floor to ceiling with hard-to-find Chucks, Air Force Ones, and imports. Around the block, past all the hoity-toity storefronts, is Capsule's couture counterpart—just in case you needed an outfit to go with your new kicks.

MY PICKS

Nick Fleehart
BEERLEAGUETALK
.COM

Podcasts, videos, a blog, and their own merch line, all for beer leaguers, by beer leaguers. Everything hockey, from the pro life to beer league struggles.

We play a beer league tourney in Toronto and they have the perfect setup.

A hotel next door to the old Maple Leaf Gardens . . .

SLEEP
HOLIDAY INN TORONTO DOWNTOWN CENTRE
30 CARLTON ST.
416.977.6655

And a party right across the street . . .

DRINK
MICK E FYNN'S
45 CARLTON ST.
416.598.0537

HISTORY
LOBLAWS
60 CARLTON ST. • 416.593.6154

No, this is not a call for a cleanup in aisle 25. The red dot on the floor of the International Foods aisle is actually the exact spot of center ice in the original Maple Leaf Gardens on the corner of Carlton and Church.

EAT
BLACK CAMEL
4 CRESCENT RD.
416.929.7518

A sandwich menu boiled down to seven variations, covering all the basic meat types plus a veggie option, with brisket and pulled pork leading the pack. Usually a line but it moves quickly, with limited seating steering you across the street to Ramsden Park.

BEER LEAGUE PICK
JOSH COOPER

PHYSICAL THERAPY
INSIDE OUT PHYSIO
1240 BAY ST.
416.925.0050
A great clinic.

SLEEP
BOND PLACE HOTEL TORONTO
65 DUNDAS ST. E
416.362.6061

A clean, efficient, subtly hip hotel around the corner from the quasi madness of Dundas Square, Times Square's well-behaved little cousin.

ARENA GARDENS

From 1912 to 1989, this was the site of Arena Gardens, the second rink to be built here. With a seating capacity of 7,500, the arena was billed as the largest in the country and was home to many professional hockey teams, including the franchise that became the Toronto Maple Leafs. Norman Albert gave the first radio broadcast of an NHL hockey game here on February 14, 1923. A Toronto team won three Stanley Cups in the building.

Arena Gardens also hosted numerous public gatherings, including political, religious, and other social events. The inaugural service of the United Church of Canada was held here in 1925, and musical legends Frank Sinatra and Glenn Miller performed here in the 1940s.

Following the Toronto Maple Leafs' move to Maple Leaf Gardens in 1931, the facility was renamed Mutual Street Arena and was used for recreational ice skating and roller skating. In 1962, the arena was renovated to add curling sheets and was renamed The Terrace. It was demolished in 1989.

HERITAGE TORONTO 2013

HISTORY
MUTUAL ST. ARENA PLAQUE
88 MUTUAL ST.

Toronto hockey lore: The year is 1931 and Maple Leaf Gardens is being rushed to completion for the start of the season. Owner Conn Smythe decides he wants to kill two birds with one stone—hire a staff that knows how to run a rink (understandable) and ensure that the Leafs' previous home would never host another professional hockey game (a bit nuts?). Solution: He offers jobs to the folks working at the old arena, but they have to accept, in person, before he heads out for lunch that day. In unison, they leave their posts and head to the construction site. Small problem, who would tend the furnace powering the rink's ice-making machinery? No one, ultimately leading to the destruction of the ice plant. How could Smythe possibly know this would happen? Lore, like most history, is hazy. What we know for a fact is that the original arena was home to the Toronto Arenas, Blueshirts, and St. Pats, in addition to being the first home of the Maple Leafs and the site of the first radio broadcast of an NHL game (1923).

ROAD TRIP PICK

ANDRE LEGASPI

DRINK
HAIR OF THE DOG

425 CHURCH ST.
416.964.2708
This laid-back pub sits diagonally across from the site of the old Gardens, with a solid house lager, along with a good selection of imports and domestics. The bar also has some stellar grub, and their brunch is definitely worth a return trip the next morning.

SLEEP
THE ANNDORE HOUSE
15 CHARLES ST. E • 416.924.1222

New boutique hotel where, along with everything else (in-house barbershop, C. O. Bigelow bath swag), you'll get the Anndore House app, which allows you to control room temperature, lighting, and room service orders through your phone.

EAT
SMOKE'S POUTINERIE
203 DUNDAS ST. E • 416.603.2873

It's early Saturday, say 3:30 a.m., and you and your crew have been up all night . . . reading, and you might need to fill your stomachs with some hearty yet traditional Canadian grub before you call it a night. So you stumble upon this tiny spot with no seating and a Poutine-only menu.

SKATE
NATHAN PHILLIPS
SQUARE
100 QUEEN ST. W

Show up with your
skates during the win-
ter months and check
it off your bucket list.
(They do rent skates, but
that's like using someone
else's toothbrush, right?)
Impress your co-skaters
with this little nugget:
In 1989, a chunk of the
recently demolished
Berlin Wall was placed
at the base of the
central arch.

EAT / DRINK
SHARK CLUB
10 DUNDAS ST. E
416.506.0753

Fifty-seven screens, plus a 90-foot sports ticker, compete with views overlooking Dundas Square. Try a Shark Burger; it's not what you think.

EAT
OZZY'S BURGERS
66 NASSAU ST. • 416.862.7983

Opened in early 2018, this cramped hole-in-the-wall serves large burgers with a focus on fresh. Apparently new, good food in Toronto means no place to sit and lines out the door (and there actually is an Ozzy). Special burgers announced on IG @ ozzysburgers. When hype meets truth, you've found your spot.

Foster Hewitt
TORONTO MAPLE LEAFS
'27–'63

"He shoots, he scores" hardly seems a phrase steeped in legend, but someone had to say it first and that someone was Foster Hewitt, broadcasting the first game from Maple Leaf Gardens when it opened in 1931. Before streaming, YouTube, ESPN, before TV itself, Hewitt honed the craft of watching a hockey game in real time and telling the story, simultaneously. Granted, he didn't have 31 rosters to memorize, and his voice—thin, nasal, and high-pitched—was by no means mesmerizing, but that may have been his secret. Even though he was broadcasting from high above the crowd in the "gondola," he had the insight to remain part of the crowd, getting excited, if not hysterical, when they did, his voice rising as theirs did in the background. The miracle, frankly, is that he never fell out of that gondola. In fact, his talent was, at the time, so unique that it was copied, literally. An announcer on another station was listening to Hewitt's and repeating it, word for word. Hewitt got wind of this and complained to the broadcasting author-ities, who in turn said they needed proof. Hewitt's plan: make up two goals, one for each team, that never hap-pened. Brilliant.

VINTAGE
SEARCH & RESCUED
184 BALDWIN ST.
416.979.2266

A spectacularly cluttered Army/Navy surplus shop, loaded with camo, aviators and beanies, and all the military accessories your band might need for the next gig. This store is a perfect illustration of Kensington Market, an eclectic neighborhood from another era, simpatico with New York City's East Village or San Francisco's Haight Ashbury. Replete with cafes, boutiques, and restaurants, tourists mix with locals, ambling the streets lined with Victorian houses. The sheer amount of Instagrammable moments will slow your pace in this self-contained bohemian ecosystem, celebrated for its fierce embrace of the countercultural fight against corporate development. Nike, for instance, attempted to open a store here but was scared away by its proud local militancy. Time will tell how long they will be able to hinder the advance of what may be inevitable gentrification, but for now, this is a must-see. Search these streets and you might even find a vintage jersey of that notorious counterculture hero, former Leaf Alexander Mogilny (okay, it wasn't *our* culture he was countering).

ROAD TRIP
PICK

ANDRE LEGASPI

PLAY / WATCH
VARSITY
ARENA

299 BLOOR ST. W

In the '70s, it was home to the Toronto Toros (WHA). Then the Toronto Planets (the short-lived Roller Hockey International) bunked here briefly in the '90s. But the Varsity Blues (OUA), the University of Toronto's hockey team, have been permanent residents of Varsity Arena from the beginning. The pillarless venue provides great sightlines which, unfortunately, aren't shown here because the rink was closed for maintenance when I stopped by.

LOCAL HISTORY

Stan Fischler

RENOWNED HOCKEY
BROADCASTER,
JOURNALIST, AND
AUTHOR RECOUNTS
THE TIME HE AND
HIS FRIENDS
**INVENTED THE
ROAD TRIP**.

It's March 1952 and the Toronto Maple Leafs, reigning Cup champs, are playing the Detroit Red Wings in the first round of the playoffs. A 19-year-old Stan Fischler, Brooklyn College student and Leaf fan, gets the inspired idea to make the pilgrimage to "the cathedral of hockey." The plan: get tickets to Game 3, Saturday night, Maple Leaf Gardens.

Challenge #1: Who's going with him? Almost immediately, his roller hockey teammate and fellow Leaf fan, Jimmy Herndon, agrees to make the trip.

Challenge #2: How to get tickets? Simple enough, even in pre-StubHub 1952. "I contacted a ticket agency in Toronto, and was able to buy two, one for me and one for Jimmy." Okay, maybe this will be easy.

Soon enough, others learn of the plan and want in. Carl Glickman, Freddy Meyer, and Jimmy Coggins didn't really care about the Leafs, but liked the idea of going up to Toronto. By the time they agreed to go, it was too late to try the ticket agency. Fischler had a plan, kind of. More on that later.

Challenge #3: How do they get there? Fischler is too young to rent a car, a plane is out of the question, and somehow a train or bus doesn't feel right. As it turns out, Glickman has an older

SLEEP NO MORE
HOTEL FORD
BAY AND DUNDAS
Opened in 1929,
demolished in 1973.

brother, Marty, who recently bought a brand-new Pontiac. "In retrospect, the question is what sane guy would lend these five shmendriks his brand-new car to drive to Toronto to watch a hockey game? I would cross-examine him for years after, how did you con your brother into this?"

So a plan is made—a plan that begins with a 3 a.m. rendezvous on Marcy Avenue in Williamsburg, and a daylong drive getting them to Toronto late Friday before Saturday night's Game 3. As they leave the city, the boys are desperate to find out the result of Game 2, played the previous night, which they all slept through in order to make their 3 a.m. meet-up. Detroit won Game 1, and a loss would put the Leafs in an obvious hole. Stopping at a diner in Elmira, Fischler spots a stack of the local newspaper, the *Elmira Times*. "I go through the pages slowly; I'm scared to find out. There it is—Red Wings won 1–0. Detroit is up 2–0."

Knowing Saturday's game is now a must-win, the tension in the car rises. After making the necessary sightseeing stop in Niagara Falls, they arrive in Toronto. "We were booked into the Hotel Ford, a two-and-a-half star hotel, not a dump," Fischler insists.

And this is when his plan to secure the three additional tickets kicks in . . . or not. Back in New York, he knew another Leaf-crazy roller hockey player, Stan Shelofsky, who was planning to go up for the game. He told Fischler that he'd be able

to get three tickets from Leaf players he knew, and they'd meet at Hotel Ford at 5 o'clock for the handoff. Fischler was skeptical, but it was his only shot. "Honestly, as we're driving up, my thought was that three of the guys would be watching from a tavern."

They get to the hotel, check in, go down to the lobby, and . . . there's Shelofsky, with the tickets. "Much better seats than what I had gotten from the ticket agent!"

Next on the agenda, head for a bar. At that time Toronto had male-only taverns, a strange concept to Fischler. In addition, he was never a beer drinker, "so it took me about two hours to finish one; meantime they had about five each, which was an astonishing thing to see." Then it's time, finally, to see the Gardens. "Carlton and Church, there it is," says Fischler.

Saturday arrives and it's game day. A strange detail might come into play if the game goes past midnight, as it had in the previous year's playoffs. At that time, the city of Toronto didn't allow sporting events to take place on a Sunday, so if a game appeared to be headed that late, it would be stopped, rescheduled, and replayed in its entirety. "We assumed that if the game had to be replayed, we wouldn't get

Marty Glickman's Pontiac a second time."

Not to worry on this night. Detroit scores first, Toronto ties it up, but from then on it was all Detroit. They win 6–2, Toronto now down 0–3. Outside the Gardens following the game, the boys wait to get autographs from the departing players, and center Max Bentley approaches them. "I can never be sure, but I think he was crying, it was a humiliating loss."

Detroit went on to sweep Toronto and then sweep Montreal for the Cup. Historical sidebar: The Red Wings' octopus tradition was birthed during the finals that year, thrown on the ice during Game 4, as a good luck charm symbolized by the cephalopod's eight tentacles (eight wins to a Cup).

"It was a long drive home. We were disheartened, but we were happy. We were there. I saw the "gondola" where Foster Hewitt was doing the games, never dreaming that I'd be broadcasting from it in 1978 for the Leafs / Islanders series."

Fischler followed up his trip to Toronto the next year with a visit to Montreal and an upclose view of the Forum. That trip, he went by air, his first time on a plane. An unparalleled decades-long career brought him to all the remaining rinks.

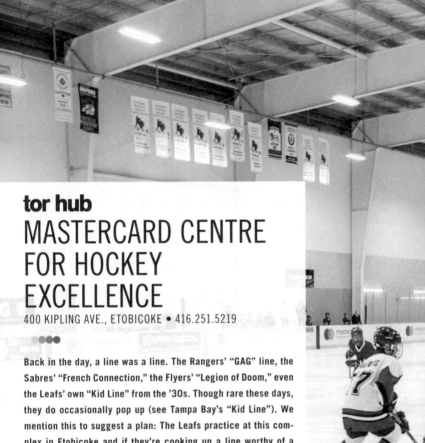

tor hub
MASTERCARD CENTRE
FOR HOCKEY
EXCELLENCE

400 KIPLING AVE., ETOBICOKE • 416.251.5219

●●●

Back in the day, a line was a line. The Rangers' "GAG" line, the Sabres' "French Connection," the Flyers' "Legion of Doom," even the Leafs' own "Kid Line" from the '30s. Though rare these days, they do occasionally pop up (see Tampa Bay's "Kid Line"). We mention this to suggest a plan: The Leafs practice at this complex in Etobicoke and if they're cooking up a line worthy of a nickname, it'll happen here. Better still, the practices are open to the public so you might get a first glance at a line that's clicking, giving you a jump on coming up with that catchy moniker. Hey, you might even see a combination the coaches miss, and make a suggestion. You won't be able to shout out your thoughts, though, because viewing isn't rinkside but from the lobby and is limited to 25. Obviously, the kids in this photo aren't pros (yet) and exactly what they were doing here at 10:30 a.m. on a school day is unclear. Oh, Canada.

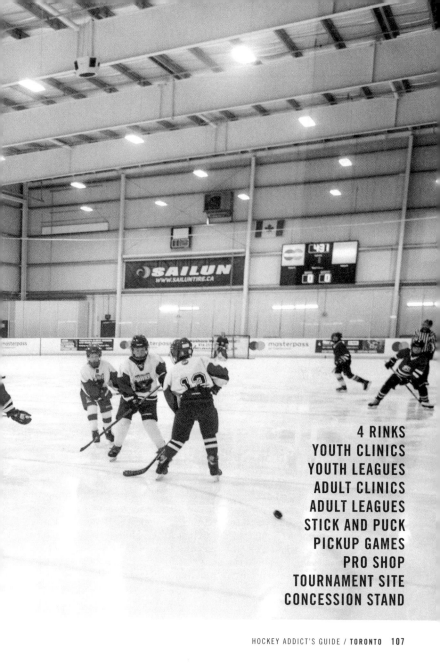

4 RINKS
YOUTH CLINICS
YOUTH LEAGUES
ADULT CLINICS
ADULT LEAGUES
STICK AND PUCK
PICKUP GAMES
PRO SHOP
TOURNAMENT SITE
CONCESSION STAND

SKATE

COLONEL SAM SMITH SKATING TRAIL

65 COLONEL SAMUEL SMITH PARK DR., ETOBICOKE • 416.392.9715

While this spot won't be confused with Ottawa's Rideau Canal, where folks strap on the skates and make their way to work, it is yet another reason to always have your wheels with you whenever you're in this city. Toronto's first outdoor skating trail, a figure-eight over 800 feet long, winds its way through an official bird sanctuary. Though we think it's a really bad idea to bring binoculars, given that skating and birdwatching seems a toxic mix, we do suggest you BYOS (Bring Your Own Skates) because there are no rentals available. Open during winter months, with free parking to go along with free skating, you'll find an outdoor fireplace and a toasty changing room inside a 19th-century heating plant. Again, why don't we all live in Canada?

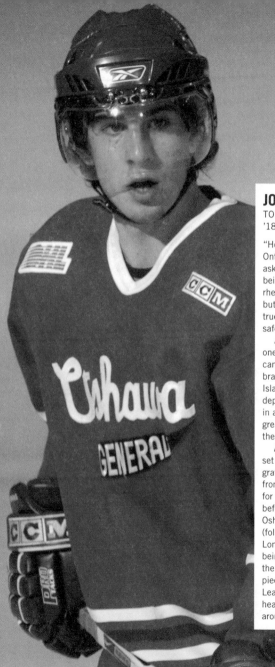

JOHN TAVARES
TORONTO MAPLE LEAFS
'18–PRESENT

"How many people from Ontario play in the NHL?" asked Mike Babcock upon being brought on as coach. A rhetorical question to be sure but his follow-up revealed his true point: "Once we make it safe, they're coming home."

And on Canada Day 2018, one did deem it safe and came home, immediately branded a traitor on Long Island. Even the recently departed Lou Lamarillo got in a shot ("John has achieved great individual success on the ice . . ."). Ouch.

A true Torontonian—one set of grandparents immigrated from Poland, the other from Portugal, Tavares played for the Marlboros of the GTHL before his time with the Oshawa Generals of the OHL (followed by a trade to the London Knights), ultimately being drafted number one by the Islanders. Is he a final piece to the puzzle in the Leaf's Cup quest or another heavy contract wrapped around their neck?

EAT & DRINK
SCHUEY'S
1130 MARTIN GROVE RD.
ETOBICOKE
416.249.1516

If Toronto was the setting for *Cheers*, this working-class roadhouse near the airport might have been the location, with jerseys hanging above the bar and every inch of wall space crammed, salon-style, with photos and memorabilia, live music, and food service until 1 a.m. Everyone *does* seem to know everyone's name.

BARBERSHOP
GREASE MONKEY BARBER
366 ROYAL YORK RD.
ETOBICOKE

This place could be mistaken for a museum celebrating retro 1950s car culture, but a closer look reveals a cash-only, old-school barbershop with a menu of services offering "head gaskets," "overhauls," and "tune-ups"—all of which bring new meaning to the phrase "chop shop."

EAT
CHABAN
872 THE QUEENSWAY
ETOBICOKE • 416.255.8222

Unassuming inside and out, this family-run spot serves up authentic Korean fare, in a space that seats about 20 and gets packed quickly. Begin with a Max Korean malt beer, go all in on the spices, and keep the water coming.

CAFFEINE
FAIR GROUNDS
3785 LAKE SHORE BLVD. W
ETOBICOKE • 416.251.2233

Ethical coffee, enough said.

GEAR
DUKE'S SOURCE FOR SPORTS
3876 BLOOR ST. W, ETOBICOKE
416.233.2011

This neighborhood hockey shop has been around long enough that folks who came in as kids are now bringing in their kids to get fitted. With equipment available in every price range, the staff points you to what you need, not what has the highest tag. Trust = priceless.

PLAY
PRINCE OF WALES RINK
1 THIRD ST., ETOBICOKE • 416.392.2489

You've seen one rink, you've seen them all, so in this case we're showing you a glimpse *from* the rink, a bucolic setting with a postcard view. Open December through February, this lakeside single sheet has the usual schedule of public skating and shinny games, and is also a great place to watch the sunrise.

SKATE
CANLAN ICE SPORTS
1120 MARTIN GROVE RD., ETOBICOKE • 416.247.5742

This organization has 16 rinks throughout Canada, seven in GTA (and a few in the US), offering youth and adult clinics, tournaments, and leagues, along with ice to rent. Last we checked, the ice at Etobicoke was going for $175–250 CAD an hour, so we got out our phones and did some quick math. Two squads of 10 means each skater pays between $12.50–8.75 CAD, and this is for a Friday night at 8:30 p.m. or a Saturday afternoon at 3:30 p.m. That averages out to $7 USD for an hour. The more complicated math involves relocating our homes, jobs, and families to take advantage of our highest priority: cheap ice time. Give us a minute, we're still working on it.

WOODY'S BURGERS
3795 LAKE SHORE BLVD. W, ETOBICOKE • 416.546.2093

You smell it before you see it. With a limited menu (always a harbinger of fine food) and huge portions, this is not the choice for a delicate eater. Tempt fate with the "Coronary" (a burger stuffed with cheese and topped with fried onions, smoked bacon, fried egg, and mayo). Wait time is no surprise as each burger is made to order, so indulge in one of their local craft beers on tap.

BEYOND THE HUB
STICKS
HOCKEYSTICKMAN SHOWROOM
5155 SPECTRUM WAY, UNIT 37, MISSISSAUGA • 905.624.2063

A thousand square feet of nothing but sticks, though the bulk of their family-run business is online (hockeystickman.com) where they've broken down the categories to Pro Stock, Hard to Find Pro Stock, Blacked Out Pro Stock, Refurbished, and Proper Flex kids' sticks.

RESOURCE
THE ADULT SAFE HOCKEY LEAGUE
ASHL.CA

Register as a team or individually in the largest adult recreational league in the world with over 62,000 playing across North America. You'll easily find your place among five skill levels, and four age brackets, with men's, women's, and coed leagues. Due to the sheer size of the organization, they start their playoffs with divisional rounds followed by facility rounds, leading all the way to the ASHL National Championship. They even have a rulebook designed specifically for adult rec hockey. The league deals with game times, refs, and stats, and all players receive insurance coverage for their time on the ice. In the Toronto area, the league plays their games at Canlan Ice Sports facilities in Etobicoke, Oakville, Oshawa, Scarborough, and York.

tor hub

SCOTIABANK ARENA

40 BAY ST.

●●●●

Unlike during the Islanders blundering move to Brooklyn's Barclays Center, this arena (until recently known as the Air Canada Centre) actually made the requisite alterations to accommodate ice. A mid-construction change in ownership led to an agreement to bring the Leafs here after initially being designed only for basketball, as a home for the Raptors. The most visionary element, though, was the creation of Legends Row, a collection of statues situated outside the venue. While NHL arenas are rich in the monument game, from Chicago's Hull and Mikita to Boston's flying Orr (Gretzky, of course, is honored with two, one each in Edmonton and LA), Toronto's is unique. In an imaginative twist, the "players" are placed around a "bench," with additions made in installments, the most recent of which was in 2017 when Charlie Conacher, Red Kelly, Frank Mahovlich, and Wendel Clark arrived, bringing the total to 14. If the on-ice Leafs fulfill any of their promise, look for the plaza to become littered with a new generation of heroes. Note to the Isles: In your new home back on Long Island, triple-check that you can fit the ice in the stadium and budget for some statues.

ROAD TRIP PICK

ANDRE LEGASPI

SWAG, ETC.

SPORT CHEK

218 YONGE ST.
416.598.3785

Not sure why you'd need to sharpen your skates in downtown Toronto, but if you work in the area or you're going to shinny at the Mattamy Athletic Centre, don't worry. This location of Canada's largest sporting goods store can take care of you with its in-house pro shop. The store itself sits at the bottom of the Eaton Centre, baiting unsuspecting tourists with Blue Jay and Maple Leaf merch.

EAT / DRINK

THE MILLER TAVERN

31 BAY ST.
416.366.5544

We'll call this upscale-rustic, with a nice assortment of surf and turf—all in all a bit rich to rush through to make puck drop, so catalog under postgame rather than pre. Also, though hip-hop-inspired cocktail menus might be passé, the Redman's Mule was on fleek.

EAT / DRINK
THE LOOSE MOOSE
146 FRONT ST. W
416.977.8840

Around the corner from
Union Station, this
two-level local institu-
tion serves 65 beers on
tap and plenty of food
options, along with live
music in their down-
stairs Antler Room.

STEAM WHISTLE BREWERY

255 BREMNER BLVD. • 416.362.2337

A native of Thornhill, Ontario, Dominic Moore has played for 10 different NHL teams over a career spanning 12 seasons. SmashFest, Moore's NHLPA-supported charity ping-pong challenge, was founded to raise awareness about concussions and rare cancers, and functioned as a fundraiser for The Katie Moore Foundation, named in honor of Dominic's wife, who passed away in January 2013. In its first six years, the summer event—attended by NHL players and alumni alike—has raised a total of $665,000 CAD, with Patrick Eaves of Anaheim crowned champion for three straight years.

Located in a brick railway roundhouse near the CN Tower, the brewery has served as the venue for SmashFest each year of the tournament. "Steam Whistle has been a great partner and a big part of the success of the event," says Moore. "I think everyone who comes here, they see the banners and they feel the vibe. It's special. If you haven't been, you've got to check it out."

—**ROB DEL MUNDO**

ROAD TRIP PICK

ANDRE LEGASPI

EAT / DRINK
REAL SPORTS BAR

15 YORK ST. • 416.815.7325

A beer at Scotiabank Arena will set you back $16 CAD and even with the exchange rate in the USD's favor, that's pretty steep. Head across the street to the Toronto version of Times Square's ESPN Zone—big screens surrounding an even bigger, Imax-style monitor beaming every conceivable sporting event.

EAT / DRINK
BOXCAR SOCIAL

235 QUEENS QUAY W. • 647.349.1210

These folks are serious, like *Portlandia* serious, with each "program" (menu) option served with a side of narrative, be it coffee, wine, beer, or whiskey. If millennial passion blossoms in the obsession to detail, welcome to an irony-free workshop where pour overs, whiskey flights, and cheese boards are all curated with similar attention. Since launching their original location in Summerhill, they've opened three others, including this one at Harbourfront with its airy, industrial feel, which in winter months, offers an extra benefit: free outdoor skating at the adjacent Natrel Rink.

THE FOX

35 BAY ST.
416.869.3535

Here, the walls drip with a hodgepodge of vintage sports equipment, from polo mallets to snowshoes, and even the occasional sweater and stick, all infused with a non-intrusive set of screens. Proximity to the arena is a main attribute, along with standard pub fare.

MY PICKS

Chris Chapman

NHL OFF-ICE OFFICIAL

Approaching his 1,000th game on duty, his night involves tabulating real-time stats: hits, give-aways, and takeaways. Away from Scotiabank Arena, he wears the referee stripes along with a whistle in Toronto's recreational leagues.

INTERVIEW BY ROB DEL MUNDO

EAT / DRINK

WILD GOOSE
5395 EGLINTON AVE. W
ETOBICOKE
416.620.6868

SHOELESS JOE'S SPORTS GRILL
1980 ST. CLAIR AVE. W
416.766.8999

JOE DOG'S
531 BRANT ST., BURLINGTON
905.632.5110

POOL

CROOKED CUE [1]
3056 BLOOR ST. W, ETOBICOKE
416.236.7736

MUSIC

BUDWEISER STAGE
909 LAKE SHORE BLVD. W
416.260.5600

DENTIST

ROYAL YORK DENTISTRY
3034 BLOOR ST. W, ETOBICOKE
416.231.0550

BARBERSHOP

SPORTCLIPS
1602 THE QUEENSWAY
ETOBICOKE
416.251.5255

DAY TRIP

NIAGARA FALLS

SHOUT OUT

MOHAWK RACETRACK
9430 GUELPH LINE, MILTON
888.675.722

1

DRINK
AMSTERDAM BREW HOUSE
245 QUEENS QUAY W
416.504.1020

Drink in the sweet views from this 14,000-square-foot lakeside brewery, restaurant, and retail space. Expect to wait for a sought-after patio seat but once you snag one, remember not to let your beer get warm as you snap endless pics—of the craft beer and the majestic lake.

BEER
LEAGUE
PICKS
JOSH COOPER

BARBERSHOP
IVAN HAIR SALON
21 VICTORIA ST.
416.364.3876
Nothing beats my 71-year-old Italian barber, Clemente, located at King and Victoria. He's a gem and is pure precision with the clippers and the straight blade.

CAFFEINE
FAHRENHEIT COFFEE
120 LOMBARD ST.
647.896.1774

MASSAGE
MASSAGE MATTERS
97 GEORGE ST.
647.340.5475

DRINK
CORNER PLACE
11 JARVIS ST.
416.850.1738

Darryl Sittler
TORONTO MAPLE LEAFS
'70–'82

A quiet leader during one of the many non-Cup stretches, Sittler often weathered drama worthy of a reality show. Example: GM Imlach, who didn't get along with Sittler's agent but couldn't move him due to his no-trade contract, out of spite, traded Sittler's best friend Lanny MacDonald, to which Darryl responded by getting a pair of scissors and cutting off the "C" from his jersey prior to a game. But on February 7, 1976, all was well, as Sittler racked up 10 points (6 G, 4 A), a record that still stands. This particular photo doesn't suggest a fast-paced tilt, as a bit of beer league calm seems to have settled in, though Bruins rookie keeper Dave Reece probably doesn't recall it that way, playing in his final NHL game. The team from Beantown didn't forget, though, as they went undefeated at the Gardens for the next three years.

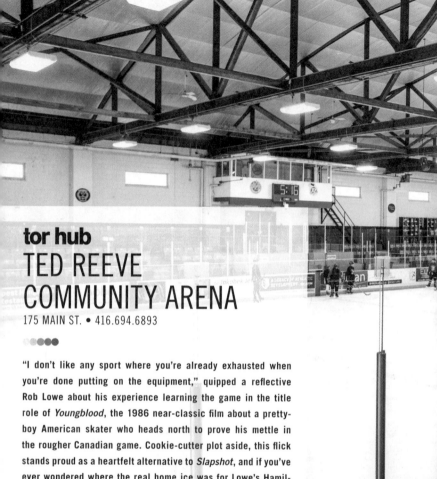

tor hub

TED REEVE
COMMUNITY ARENA

175 MAIN ST. • 416.694.6893

"I don't like any sport where you're already exhausted when you're done putting on the equipment," quipped a reflective Rob Lowe about his experience learning the game in the title role of *Youngblood*, the 1986 near-classic film about a pretty-boy American skater who heads north to prove his mettle in the rougher Canadian game. Cookie-cutter plot aside, this flick stands proud as a heartfelt alternative to *Slapshot*, and if you've ever wondered where the real home ice was for Lowe's Hamilton Mustangs, you've found it. A true community rink, built after a few warm winters became a catalyst for the construction of some indoor ice, completed in 1954 and named for Ted Reeve, a local sports legend turned journalist and a vocal supporter of the new arena. Run by volunteers, the rink offers a non-competitive house league, a semi-competitive select program, a competitive GTHL program, pickup games, and ice rental.

YOUTH CLINICS
YOUTH LEAGUES
ADULT CLINICS
ADULT LEAGUES
PICK UP GAMES
CONCESSION STAND

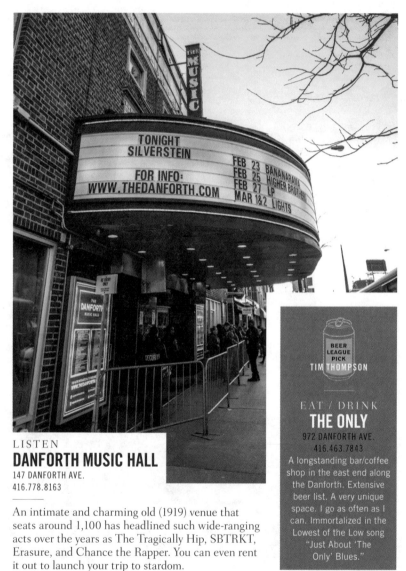

LISTEN
DANFORTH MUSIC HALL
147 DANFORTH AVE.
416.778.8163

An intimate and charming old (1919) venue that seats around 1,100 has headlined such wide-ranging acts over the years as The Tragically Hip, SBTRKT, Erasure, and Chance the Rapper. You can even rent it out to launch your trip to stardom.

BEER LEAGUE PICK
TIM THOMPSON

EAT / DRINK
THE ONLY
972 DANFORTH AVE.
416.463.7843
A longstanding bar/coffee shop in the east end along the Danforth. Extensive beer list. A very unique space. I go as often as I can. Immortalized in the Lowest of the Low song "Just About 'The Only' Blues."

EAT / DRINK
MAPLE LEAF TAVERN
955 GERRARD ST. E
416.465.0955

Back in the day, in order to serve food and call yourself a "tavern," your establishment was required to have a minimum number of beds available to road-weary travelers. We'd like to request that this law be thrown back on the books. After downing a few Old-Fashioneds (made with Forty Creek, Rittenhouse Rye, Smoked Maple Syrup, and De Groff's Bitters) and diving into our 16 oz. mutton chops, we found ourselves overwhelmed—the heat radiating from the wood-fired grill washed over us, along with the dark wood and leather-detailed interior, leading to a deep and urgent need to crawl upstairs to our lodging for the night. But, born in the wrong century, we spilled out onto the street, making our way somewhere.

EAT
THE REAL JERK
842 GERRARD ST. E
416.463.6055
1004 KINGSTON RD.
416.690.8752

Next time you're watching Rihanna and Drake's 2016 "Work" video (the Director X version), you might notice that there are a few shots of food (2:10–2:15). It does look good, but honestly, the crowd doesn't seem all that concerned with it, though they do seem to be having a fine time. What you might want to remember is the fact that it was filmed at the Real Jerk, offering up legit Caribbean cuisine in a true West Indian atmosphere.

SKATE
GREENWOOD PARK
150 GREENWOOD AVE.
416.392.7804

Playing under the stars has its romance, but what about when the weather won't cooperate? In 2013, the town elders, in their tireless effort to keep folks on skates, constructed the city's first outdoor covered rink, not only providing protection from the elements but also extending the skating season (because the ice is shielded from the sun). Public skates and pickup games fill the winter schedule, while in the summer, in addition to ball hockey, basketball is offered as retractable nets are put in place. And yes, that's a winding skating path on the right of the photo, because, well, why not?

SWAG
PRO LEAGUE SPORTS COLLECTIBLES
1957 QUEEN ST. E
416.699.2097

Small mom & pop carrying sports apparel, from snapbacks to custom team uniforms.

1

Andrew Podnieks

MOYDART PRESS

A prolific author and publisher specializing in the world of hockey, he has over 45 titles to his credit, including a series based on the photo archives of the Hockey Hall of Fame.

Favorite bookstores—it's difficult these days to list because so many of the small ones have closed, but a great small one:

BOOK CITY (1)

348 DANFORTH AVE.
416.469.9997
WITH 3 ADDITIONAL
LOCATIONS:
1950 QUEEN ST. E
416.698.1444
2354 BLOOR ST. W
416.961.4496
1430 YONGE ST.
416.926.0749

Also excellent:

THE INDIGO

55 BLOOR ST. W • 416.925.3536
I play shinny with friends two to three times a week. The core group has played together for 25 to 30 years. Because it has an NHL and International pad, and the ice is usually in great condition, this is my favorite rink.

UCC (WILLIAM WILDER)

200 LONSDALE RD.
416.488.1125

EAT / DRINK

RALLY SPORTS BAR + SMOKEHOUSE

1660 O'CONNOR DR.
NORTH YORK
416.551.7356

Plenty of screens and wood-smoked barbecue options in an atmosphere that, at this point, could be called a throwback, to a time before every menu item had a story and a hefty price.

COFFEE, ETC.
PRESS
2442 DANFORTH AVE.
647.352.5200

Crate diggers and bibliophiles have one goal in common: to unearth the serendipitous gem. How sweet, then, to come up for air and to be greeted by a fine macchiato, along with a broccoli and cheddar scone. But beware, this pretense-free community hub, opened in 2015, might just turn your quick coffee pitstop into another lost day as you scour their shelves and bins for used books and new/used vinyl.

DRINK
LINSMORE TAVERN
1298 DANFORTH AVE. • 416.466.5130

East York institution dating back to the '30s, a proud dive where time stands still—this isn't retro, it's old. Interesting characters, pool and dart leagues, karaoke, and an eclectic range of live music acts, known for its lineup of cover bands.

BEER
LEAGUE
PICKS
ROB SCRUTON

EAT / DRINK
SMOKE SIGNALS BBQ
1242 DUNDAS ST. W
416.588.7408
Awesome BBQ resto.
SCHUEY'S
1130 MARTIN GROVE RD.
ETOBICOKE
416.249.1516
Postgame
hockey-themed bar.
P.G. CLUCKS
610 COLLEGE ST.
416.539.8224
Fried chicken!

SKATE / SNOW
SANCTION
330 STEELES AVE. W
THORNHILL
905.738.8644

COMICS
SILVER SNAIL
329 YONGE ST.
416.593.0889

BARBERSHOP
CROW'S NEST
2 KENSINGTON AVE.
647.346.4333

SKATE PARK
SKATE LOFT
763 WARDEN AVE.
647.688.9568

ROAD TRIP PICK

ANDRE LEGASPI

E A T

DETROIT EATERY

389 DANFORTH AVE.
416.461.0136

Even though it would make more sense for this hockey haven to be in a city like, oh, Detroit or even Windsor, Ontario, it doesn't seem out of place here in Greektown. Despite the sea of red dotted with winged wheels, hockey takes precedence over allegiance. The waiters are always quick to point out the Hanson brothers' autographs on the wall or to talk about the state of the NHL.

E AT

THE WREN

1382 DANFORTH AVE.
647.748.1382

Authentic Southwestern fare, along with 12 rotating Ontario craft beers on tap, served up in a rustic salvage-yard-style setting.

BEYOND THE HUB

EQUIPMENT
JUST HOCKEY
900 DON MILLS RD.
416.445.5700

For over 30 years, this locally owned franchise has offered a hyper-loyal customer base every level of equipment, including goalie, and a full set of services: blade sharpening and contouring, skate stretching, glove repair, custom team jerseys, and equipment sanitization. Affiliated with the Source For Sports organization, they have access to equipment from the big brands at a lower wholesale price by being connected to over 150 other independently owned stores across Canada (see also Duke's Source for Sports on page 73).

MY PICKS

Natalie Spooner

TORONTO FURIES,
THE CANADIAN
WOMEN'S HOCKEY
LEAGUE

A native of Scarborough, Ontario, Natalie is a member of an exclusive women's triple-gold club, having an Olympic Gold medal, a women's World Championship Gold medal, and a Clarkson Cup title to her credit. In 2014, Spooner somehow had time to team up with fellow Canadian Olympian Meaghan Mikkelson to compete on *The Amazing Race Canada*.

What are your favorite memories of growing up in Scarborough?
I always used to think that **Ted Reeve** was the farthest rink; I watched my brothers play there but it turns out it really wasn't that far. I played my minor hockey in Durham West, outside of Pickering/Ajax, farther east.

**INTERVIEW BY
ROB DEL MUNDO**

How satisfying is it to play for the Toronto Furies (drafted in 2012)?
It was a dream come true to be drafted and to be able to play in my hometown to stay close to family, but also to know that I play for the city I grew up in, really amazing. I love Toronto.

*What makes **Master-Card Centre** a great home rink?*
It's super cool that both the Leafs and the Marlies practice there. And for the Furies to get our own locker room, and a place to call home, is really special.

Favorite place to take a visiting friend/relative?
I'd probably take my friends to the **CN Tower**. I always feel like that's something that people who come from far away [would like] to see; people always want to come right downtown and I think there's a lot to do around there, see a Leafs game or a Jays game, or a Raptors game. There are a lot of options.

#ANYTHINGFORHO

Do you get to attend a lot of sporting events?
Not really because our hockey schedule is really busy. I try to get to at least one Leafs game a year, if we have some time off.

Any favorite place to go after the game?
I've been to **Real Sports** quite a bit. When I was on *The Amazing Race Canada* I hosted viewing parties at Real Sports every night that the show was on. It was pretty fun to get everybody together and watch the show with them.

SOCHI OLYMPIC GOLD MEDALIST NATALIE SPOONER TRIES OUT THE ICE ON THE ROOFTOP HOCKEY RINK BUILT FOR A MOLSON CANADIAN AD CAMPAIGN CALLED "ANYTHING FOR HOCKEY" ON JANUARY 18, 2016.

tor hub
THE SPORT GALLERY
15 TANK HOUSE LANE • 416.861.8514

●●●●

With an additional location in Vancouver and a recently opened outlet in Boston's Faneuil Hall, this spot has a compelling history connected to, of all things, a magazine. In print for over 50 years, the monthly *SPORT* magazine was the first to capture the magic of sports in large, full-color imagery, with editorial focused not on the scores but on the stories and the aesthetic. Its run ended in 2000, but the title was brought to new life when Wayne Parrish, a former sports writer, was hired by Post Media, owner of the photo archives of the magazine, to open a gallery space to feature the images of the magazine's collection at this location in Toronto's Distillery District. This eventually led to a bigger idea: an apparel and accessory business, with brands designing products directly inspired by the images—pretty much anything you can throw a logo and colorway onto.

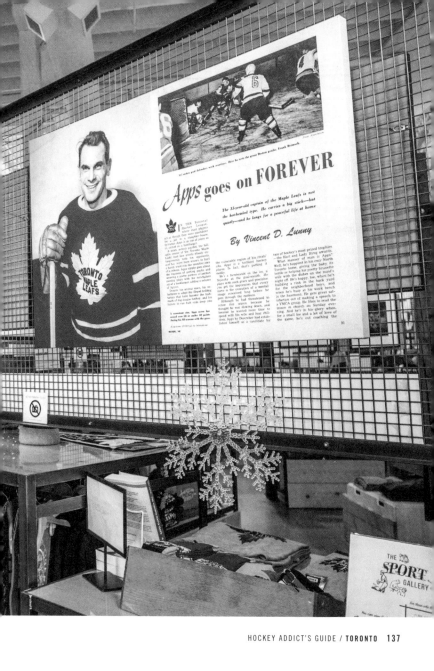

ROAD TRIP PICK

ANDRE LEGASPI

CAFFEINE
ARENA COFFEE BAR
15 TANK HOUSE LANE
416.861.8514

While there is no shortage of places to grab a coffee in the Distillery area, only one lets you do it while taking in some hockey history. Located at the entrance to The Sport Gallery, this in-house cafe offers a curated selection while you admire vintage sports photography and grainy footage of Original Six teams.

SLEEP
THE BROADVIEW HOTEL
106 BROADVIEW AVE.
416.362.8439

A landmark structure, originally built in 1891, was until recently the home of Jilly's, an infamous local strip club. Reborn as a luxury boutique hotel with 58 rooms and great rooftop bar with stunning views, you can find other nods to the building's past, not just its name (broad view, really?). For instance, one room contains an original stripper pole from Jilly's, a source of conversation, if not inspiration, for some lucky guests.

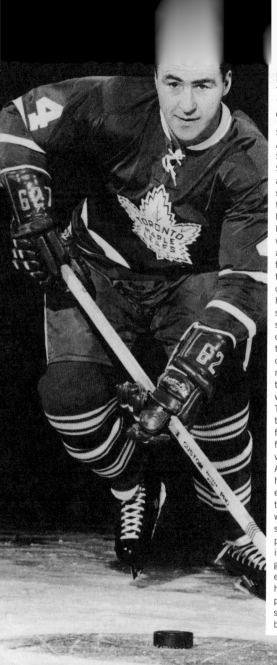

Red Kelly

TORONTO MAPLE LEAFS
'59–'67,
COACH '73–'77

Somebody make this movie: A local farm boy from nearby Simcoe gets into Leaf-factory St. Michael's only with his alumni father's help, and shows up late because he has to get the crops in. Ignored by the home team ("He won't last 20 games"), he signs with the Red Wings, where as a defenseman he wins the first-ever Norris along with four Cups. Detroit gives up on him when it's announced he played the previous season with a broken ankle, so he signs with the Leafs, only to be told after signing that he's being switched to center, which he does with no complaint and goes on to win another four Cups with his new team. While in Toronto, he wins election to the Canadian Parliament, forcing him to fly back and forth to Ottawa to cast his votes and to play his games. After his playing career, he goes into coaching and eventually winds up behind the Leafs' bench, under which, in a 1976 playoff series against the Flyers, he places pyramids because he is convinced of their energy-generating powers. Apparently, his daughter had cured her headaches by placing a pyramid under her bed. The script will sell itself, if anyone believes it.

ROAD TRIP PICK

ANDRE LEGASPI

SKATE
UNDERPASS SKATEPARK

29 LOWER RIVER ST.

Despite the squeaky-clean image of Toronto, there are a few "grittier" parts of the city. One such place is the Underpass Skatepark near the Distillery District. Developed by Waterfront Toronto in hopes of revitalizing the area, the spray-painted pillars aren't exactly examples of true urban angst; it has nonetheless been a boon to skaters in the city. Even the nearby residents have benefitted. At night, while LED lights illuminate the ledges, rails, and mini-ramps, they also provide extra visibility and safety in the West Don Lands neighborhood.

BEER LEAGUE PICK
JOSH COOPER

EAT
CHERRY STREET BAR-B-QUE
275 CHERRY ST.
416.461.5111

THE FUTURE
QUAYSIDE DEVELOPMENT
SIDEWALK TORONTO
PARLIAMENT SLIP, EAST BAYFRONT

We recently got our hands on a 170-page proposal to the city of Toronto to partner with Sidewalk Labs (an urban innovation company owned by Google's parent company Alphabet) on a new model for urban life to be developed on a 12-acre plot on the waterfront east of the Gardiner Expressway. Following a close inspection, we found no mention of new hockey rinks in their plan, and our radar was on alert. Intended to be "the world's first neighborhood built from the internet up," as Sidewalk describes it, among the many mind-boggling components will be the ability to alert residents when an Adirondack chair on the waterfront becomes free to use, or as we like to say, a solution in search of a problem. Let's be clear: we're all for progress, big data, and the future in general, but if you're really the big kahuna of the innovation world, Google, let's make sure your geniuses stay focused on providing solutions to the truly vexing issues of our time: 1. Bad ice. 2. Blind refs. 3. That smell. 4. Ringers. 5. Or maybe just get us a goalie for tonight's game. We've put calls in to voice our concerns, but have yet to hear back.

MY PICKS

Mike Wilson

ULTIMATE
LEAFS FAN

Having assembled the greatest trove of hockey treasures on the planet (aside from the Hockey Hall of Fame), Mike Wilson has one request: don't refer to him as a "collector."

"I think of myself as a preserver of history," says Wilson. "I consider myself the gatekeeper to the legacy of the Maple Leafs through the artifacts." In a frenzied market in which the prices of collectibles have skyrocketed, he is loath to possess an item solely based on its commercial value.

Known as the Ultimate Leafs Fan, Wilson amassed enough memorabilia over the past few decades to display the collection in the basement of his Toronto home, an underground museum-like man cave simply referred to as "The Room."

Visitors were amazed at the plethora of items on display, ranging from an authentic

turnstile from Maple Leaf Gardens, to the original dressing room door emblazoned with the Leafs logo and the words "Authorized Personnel Only." Also on hand was the stick rack from the hallway at the fabled arena at Carlton Street where countless Leafs stored their twigs. Among his previously unearthed gems: the long-lost 1962 Stanley Cup banner

that used to hang in Maple Leaf Gardens.

In preparation for retirement and downsizing, Wilson recently sold most of the 1,700 pieces to the Canadian Museum of History in Gatineau, Quebec, near Ottawa.

"It's about time, place, and history. One looks at a piece and it immediately takes them to that moment, and whatever memory may be triggered."

EAT / DRINK
THE DUCHESS OF MARKHAM
53 MAIN ST. N, MARKHAM
905.294.3181
I play hockey four times a week in Markham and this is the unofficial clubhouse for guys to gather after games. Comfortable atmosphere, fantastic service. I love going to the Duch to talk hockey or sports in general. Summer patio is second to none.

INTERVIEW BY ROB DEL MUNDO

THE POUR HOUSE
182 DUPONT ST.
416.967.7687
Local pub. Usually go with a few friends to watch a game.

MASSAGE
M.O.A. LIVING WELLNESS
652 SPADINA AVE.
647.247.6004
Works magic with beat-up bodies.

PLAY
MARKHAM CENTENNIAL
8600 MCCOWAN RD.
UNIONVILLE
905.294.6111
The CWHL Clarkson Cup final was hosted there for three straight years ending in 2015.

CANLAN ICE SPORTS (MARKHAM)
3552 VICTORIA PARK AVE.
416.497.4545

ROAD TRIP PICK

ANDRE LEGASPI

EAT & DRINK
RADICAL ROAD BREWING CO.

1177 QUEEN ST. E
647.794.7909

Though it's only been around a couple of years, this place has already established itself as one of Toronto's best breweries. Take the short streetcar ride down Queen Street and order either the Yuzu Pale Ale or Slingshot (a steam beer).

SURF GEAR
SURF THE GREATS
276 CARLAW AVE., UNIT 215
647.479.8969

"Surf is where you find it," according to surfing legend Gerry Lopez—a.k.a. Mr. Pipeline—and nowhere is this more true than on the Great Lakes. Yes, that big water you're always bumping into, Lake Ontario, is one of the five "Greats," and the GTA has its own mecca for the local surf crowd, a tight-knit community always keeping an eye out for the next wave. They stock all the gear you'll need, in addition to their lineup of workshops and lessons. In fact, they run the only surf school with International Surfing Association–certified instructors on the Great Lakes. So now you're wondering, when's the best time to go? Fall, apparently, brings the optimal conditions, as the colder air flows over the warmer water (we'd bore you with the physics, but we can't locate the ~~napkin~~ Moleskine containing that day's notes).

Tim Thompson

FILMMAKER, FORMER MAJOR JUNIOR & MINOR PRO

"The Maple Leaf hockey club have been champions, and they will be champions again," vows King Clancy on the center ice screen at the ACC, and for the next five minutes, the crowd is treated to a montage of Leafs highlights through the years, all the vision of the video's creator, Tim Thompson.

Following his on-ice career, Thompson took his talent to the film industry, where he eventually secured a high-profile gig: making videos for *Hockey Night in Canada*, a post he held for six seasons.

"Brendan Shanahan told me he saw people with tears in their eyes at one point," says Thompson, the native Torontonian and long-time Leafs fan. "It was really nice how much it touched people. This team means so much to so many people here."

EAT / DRINK

BELLWOODS BREWERY (1)

124 OSSINGTON AVE.
My local bar. An amazing craft brewpub, in a very unique space. They make some of the best, and most interesting, beer around, and their food is always creative and delicious.

UNION (2)

72 OSSINGTON AVE.
416.850.0093
A bustling spot on Ossington. They thrive on organic and local food. Great atmosphere and the meat is phenomenal.

REPOSADO

136 OSSINGTON AVE.
416.532.6474
A tequila bar in a loft-like setting, with a quaint back patio. Their margaritas are like none I've ever had, and you'll often catch some live music, or Sean Dean from the Sadies spinning vinyl there.

BOLT FRESH BAR (3)

1170 QUEEN ST. W
416.588.8103
A great little vegan takeout place along Queen West. Energizing, healthy food. Their burrito bowl and chocolate thunder smoothie are constants for me.

GRAND ELECTRIC

1330 QUEEN ST. W
416.627.3459
Gourmet tacos in the forever eclectic Parkdale. The back patio is really nice. It often gets very busy, but the food is well worth the wait.

LISTEN

THE DAKOTA TAVERN

249 OSSINGTON AVE.
416.850.4579
Another frequent stop for me. It's run by musicians, and there are always interesting shows there. Like the Cameron House, you never know

INTERVIEW BY ROB DEL MUNDO

3

ROTATE THIS!
186 OSSINGTON AVE.
416.504.8447

PLAY
NORTH TORONTO MEMORIAL ARENA
174 ORCHARD VIEW BLVD.
416.485.0301
The place I grew up playing hockey in. It's in Eglinton park, a few blocks from Yonge and Eglinton. A very community-oriented rink that is impeccably maintained. The best ice in the city, bar none. Gary Roberts once said "it's a pleasure to skate on this ice." I couldn't agree more. Eric Lindros and I started a skate there in 1999 that continues to this day.

who just might pop in there, too. My favorite memory was for Wayne Petti's (from Cuff the Duke/Grey Lands) 30th birthday. The night ended with Sarah Harmer and Greg Keelor singing "Lost Together" to Wayne.

MASSEY HALL
178 VICTORIA ST.
416.872.4255
The grand cathedral of live music in the city. I've seen some monumental concerts there. A beautiful, majestic sounding room, with a lot of ghosts.

WATCH
THE ROYAL
608 COLLEGE ST.
416.466.4400
A great art deco theater in the heart of Little Italy. Rotating selection of older movies, and they are starting to have a lot more live music. I made a documentary about five songwriters in Toronto

called *Born To It*, that premiered there. It's a special place for me.

SHOP
KENSINGTON MARKET
I walk around the city a lot. I get tons of ideas, and inspiration for my work from it. Kensington is one of the great areas to go and get lost in. Interesting stores and restaurants, and the people watching never ceases to amaze. You see snapshots of so many different lives in there.

VINYL
SONIC BOOM
215 SPADINA AVE.
416.532.0334
I'm a music junkie, and listen to it all day, every day. For my vinyl collection, I frequent these two quite a bit—always a good time roaming the aisles and poring over the collections for what to buy next.

SHOUT OUT
THE ISLANDS
A beautiful sanctuary just a quick ferry ride away. A wonderful view of the city, yet it seems like it's so far away.

DAY TRIP
MUSKOKA
Cottage country, about two hours north of Toronto. I've spent every summer of my life up in Muskoka. My family has a cottage on Lake Rosseau. The area is simply one of the most beautiful places on the planet. Swimming, boating, hiking, beautiful little towns, with gorgeous views.

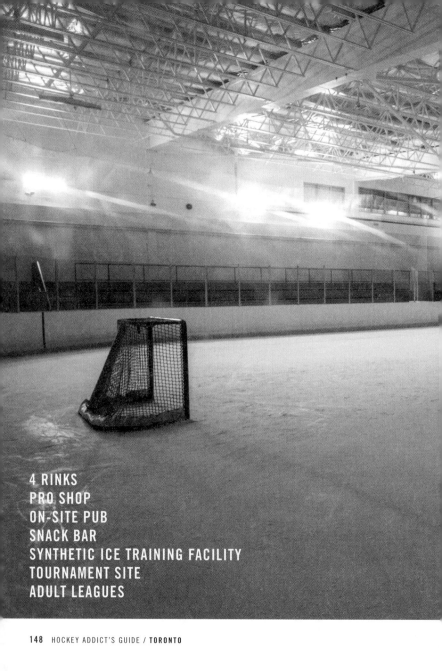

4 RINKS
PRO SHOP
ON-SITE PUB
SNACK BAR
SYNTHETIC ICE TRAINING FACILITY
TOURNAMENT SITE
ADULT LEAGUES

GEAR
**CHESSWOOD
ARENA
PRO SHOP**

Ask for Mark and you'll
get a wicked skate
sharpening. Tell him
"Coach Liz" sent ya.

tor hub
CHESSWOOD ARENA

4000 CHESSWOOD DR., NORTH YORK • 416.630.8114

A true staple of the North York community, this complex is a
beehive of activity, from pickup games and tournaments to
adult and youth leagues. Neither a creaky charm-loaded barn
nor a cutting-edge next-generation facility, it's exactly what
it needs to be. Among its other amenities, this place has the
essentials—a bar and four NHL-sized pads, with ice surfaces
powered by an upgraded refrigeration system, thanks to a part-
nership with the local power company to become more energy
efficient. In the old-is-new category, remember that as you lum-
ber down the stairs to get from the changing rooms to the rink,
what you're really doing is cardio.

GEAR
MAJER HOCKEY
4610 DUFFERIN ST.
NORTH YORK
416.736.7444

They offer equipment for sale on their Ebay store, including Pro return items, but if you're timing your visit to their brick and mortar, they hold an annual end-of-season sale in May.

BEYOND THE HUB

PLAY
WESTWOOD ARENA
90 WOODBINE DOWNS BLVD.
ETOBICOKE
416.675.7604

(Twin) sister rink to
Chesswood Arena but
with five ice surfaces.

RESOURCE
HOCKEYTORONTO.COM

Crazy deep site run by a guy you just might recognize if you've watched *The Love Guru* about a thousand times. Bruce Tennant—the local guru of all things hockey in Toronto—refs games, organizes leagues, places people on teams, and at clinics and open skates. His phone constantly buzzes with folks looking for available Leafs or Marlies tickets or asking for details on a kids' summer clinic. Sign up for his email newsletter and your hockey needs will be satisfied. Case in point: During the filming of Mike Myers' quirky 2008 flick (an attempt at comedy in the merging of the disparate worlds of Hindu spiritualism and Maple Leaf Cup ambitions), a skater was needed to play a ref in the hockey scenes filmed at the then Air Canada Centre. In this particular case, Tennant cast himself, in addition to assisting the producers on other hockey-related needs for the movie.

BEER LEAGUE PICKS
TAYLOR DINNER

EAT / DRINK
TOM & JERRY'S BISTRO

17335 YONGE ST.
NEWMARKET
905.853.2345
Local wing joint that is always generous with hockey team sponsorships.

SNEAKERS SPORTS BAR

18025 YONGE ST.
NEWMARKET
905.235.5517
A Newmarket staple for as long as I can remember! Beer is always cold, with pool, ping-pong, and air hockey.

WORKOUT
PEAK PEFORMANCE

135 INDUSTRIAL PKWY. N
AURORA
Hockey-specific training, owned by Peter Daija.

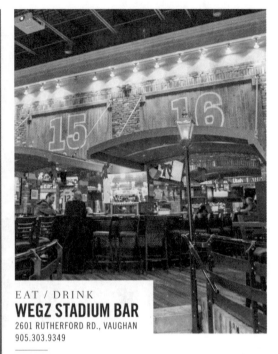

EAT / DRINK
WEGZ STADIUM BAR

2601 RUTHERFORD RD., VAUGHAN
905.303.9349

Being located outside the center of the city allows for a 23,000-square-foot cavernous corporate hunting lodge, a large and loud venue with an array of seating options and screen sizes.

SKATE
EMERY VILLAGE HOCKEY TRAINING FACILITY

5601 STEELES AVE. W, #12, NORTH YORK
647.692.7465

Designed for customized group instruction, two half-sized rinks along with state-of-the-art recording equipment, including rinkside viewing monitors that allow coaches to make immediate adjustments during on-ice sessions.

SWEATERS
GITCH
SPORTSWEAR
1140 SHEPPARD AVE. W
416.841.9104

Locally designed and
produced custom subli-
mated uniforms, along
with hoodies, sweatpants,
shorts, hats, and bags.

NEW SUBWAY STATIONS
DOWNSVIEW PARK

During our time in "T-Dot," we didn't see a whole lot of skaters taking the subway, but late 2017 did see the opening of six new stations as an extension of the 1 Northbound Vaughan line. So you can now take the train to Chesswood Arena (a brisk 10-minute walk) and Scotiabank Pond (a brisker 20 minute). Whether anyone will actually do this remains to be seen, as both rinks offer ample free parking and most up here seem to have cars, though complaining about the traffic is a common local refrain. Anyway, pardon the excuse for a nice photo and an appeal for the benefits of mass transit.

TRAIN
TORONTO SKATING LAB
3984 CHESSWOOD DR., NORTH YORK • 416.499.4300

Your stride needs work, as does your knee bend. Everyone says so. Solution: Make an appointment and jump on this treadmill. You put in the sweat, they'll add the science. Something called Kinesiology. We looked it up, but we still don't know what it is. They do.

MEMORABILIA
A.J. SPORTS WORLD
2720 STEELES AVE. W, CONCORD
888.207.1110

You have a perfect spot in your man cave for a Borje Salming autographed hockey jersey and you have two choices: Buy a clean #21 and hang around the HHOF, hoping he strolls by (like he did on our visit) *or* head here and get all wide-eyed over their endless collection of autographed swag.

GEAR
PRO HOCKEY LIFE
1 BASS PRO MILLS DR., UNIT C3
VAUGHAN
905.669.9088

Websites might offer all the gear, but not high ceilings, wide aisles, and sheer joy. Expect to gasp when you enter here, and then supress the urge to run wild, childlike, in the biggest big box of all. Whether you buy anything or not, you need to make the trek up to Vaughan to waste hours wandering through this wonderland, jaw on the floor, as you pass every size of every brand of every piece of equipment you've ever spent hours oogling over online. But as you do, your thoughts will eventually settle on the one mistake you've made today: the car in the parking lot is way too small.

GEAR

PLAY IT AGAIN SPORTS

5863 YONGE ST., NORTH YORK
416.222.5713
ADDITIONAL LOCATIONS:
2488 GERRARD ST. E
SCARBOROUGH
773 THE QUEENSWAY
ETOBICOKE

If you have kids, then you know that if you feed them regularly, they tend to grow, which means they outgrow their skates (and other equipment) pretty quickly. With 43 stores in Canada (and over 400 across the US), this is the largest sporting goods resale franchise in North America. All locations are individually owned and operated, selling new equipment as well, but used is their bread and butter, going for about half the price as new. In addition, they have a good rep for skate sharpening.

PLAY
SCOTIABANK POND
57 CARL HALL RD., NORTH YORK • 416.398.1862

This modern addition to the Chesswood/Westwood family has four NHL-sized rinks (with heated floors for spectators!) but be forewarned: Given the recent renaming of Air Canada Centre to the Scotiabank Arena, you'll need to be really specific when setting your GPS.

RESOURCE

TORONTO.SPORTSOCIAL.CLUB
416.781.4263

Meet new friends and then destroy them in a wide variety of sports, all organized by this group, which arranges adult leagues and events in hockey (ball and ice) and, additionally, basketball, dodgeball, football, golf and, of course, curling, among others. Sign up individually or as a team and get discounts at recommended bars and venues.

BEYOND THE HUB

GEAR
HOCKEY LION RICHMOND HILL
1285 ELGIN MILLS RD. E #21
RICHMOND HILL
905.508.5975
ADDITIONAL LOCATION:
6050 HIGHWAY 7 EAST, UNIT 4
MARKHAM

Full-service pro shop, handling every level of play.

PLAY
THE HANGAR AT DOWNSVIEW PARK

75 CARL HALL RD.
NORTH YORK
647.260.1560

Unless you enjoy playing ball hockey in the street, chasing the ball underneath parked cars . . . in the rain . . . at night, you might want to check out this place. Located just behind Scotiabank Pond, this indoor ball hockey rink is part of "The Hangar" complex at Downsview Park, a retrofitted structure that originally housed the manufacturing of military aircraft, including the famous Mosquito fighter-bomber. Also on the premises are four indoor soccer fields, two multisport courts, and three outdoor full-sized, artificial turf soccer fields.

ACKNOWLEDGMENTS

This guide was made by a team, some home players and some visiting. Toronto native Rob Del Mundo helped out from his hometown (see his picks below), while Andre Legaspi made the road trip up from NYC. In addition, some local beer leaguers chipped in: Josh Cooper, Tim Thompson, Liz Pead, Steven Ellis, Rob Scruton, and Taylor Dinner. Ian Peters, a Toronto native transplanted to NYC, gave his guidance. In addition, thanks go out to Ann Treistman and the crew at The Countryman Press for thinking this book might work. For all their help in putting this guide together, acknowledgment goes out to Erin Dobo, Greg Collins, John Sanful, Bruce Bennett, Stan Fischler, and Jaimie Korelitz at Getty Images. For putting up with me during the production of this book, acknowledgment goes out to the family: JBS, MSG, and TRG.

BEER LEAGUE PICKS
ROB DEL MUNDO

FAVORITE RESTAURANTS

MAKI SUSHI
45 WICKSTEED AVE.
416.696.1258
Their all-you-can-eat sushi menu is outstanding. They also have a great selection of appetizers, including their amazing squid rings.

GRAZIE
2373 YONGE ST.
416.488.0822
A fantastic Italian restaurant in midtown. I highly recommend the Nonna Franca: spaghetti with anchovy paste and a pine nuts and raisins mix.

FAVORITE PRO SHOP

JUST HOCKEY
900 DON MILLS RD.
416.445.5700
Staff is always helpful, knowledgeable, and thorough, right down to the last screw that keeps falling off my helmet.

FAVORITE BAR

HEMINGWAY'S
142 CUMBERLAND ST.
416.968.2828
A mainstay deep in the heart of Yorkville, the rooftop patio is the place to be on a summer night.

FAVORITE RINK

ST. MICHAEL'S COLLEGE SCHOOL ARENA
1515 BATHURST ST.
YORK
It's so rich in tradition with over 100 years of history, including the junior careers of Leafs legends Dave Keon and Frank Mahovlich. The only drawback is that, if my beer league team suffers a blowout loss, I feel the eyes on the banners of the 14 Hockey Hall of Fame graduates staring down at me disappointment.

INDEX

INDEX

INDEX

INDEX